ESSEX

100%
ESSEX

DOING IT THE ESSEX WAY

WENDY ROBY

Illustrations by
Andrew Pinder

Michael O'Mara Books Limited

First published in Great Britain in 2010 by
Michael O'Mara Books Limited
9 Lion Yard
Tremadoc Road
London SW4 7NQ

A CIP catalogue record for this book is available from the British Library.

Papers used by Michael O'Mara Books Limited are natural, recyclable products made from wood grown in sustainable forests. The manufacturing processes conform to the environmental regulations of the country of origin.

ISBN: 978-1-84317-614-5

1 3 5 7 9 10 8 6 4 2

www.mombooks.com

Designed and typeset by K DESIGN, Somerset

Illustrations by Andrew Pinder

Printed and bound in Great Britain by
CPI Cox & Wyman, Reading, RG1 8EX

Contents

Introduction

Welcome to Essex, The Glamorous County. May this book be your guide to all things 'major' – from how to make a sausage plait to how to beautify your noo-noo, through fashion tips for girls and boys, to Essex career advice – and much more besides.

From the world's most covetable watches to the ultimate flash cars, warning signs for a tan too far to the must-be-seen places to hang out, every aspect of the full-thrust, full-on Essex life is explored, catalogued, celebrated and shared.

This is Essex. We do things *fabulously* here.

'As far as I'm concerned, anything LA can do, Basildon can do better.'

Denise Van Outen, Essex Girl extraordinaire, speaking in *The Sun*

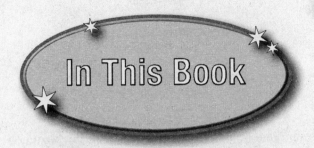

In This Book

Before we begin, a word in your ear about some aspects of this book. Dotted throughout this celebration of all things Essex, you will find the following:

Essex Lingo

Language in Essex has moved on quite some way from the 'loadsamoney' clichés of the eighties. So you need to learn the lingo if you want to pass for a truly modern Essex Girl or Boy. Always remember that famous Latin phrase ...

EPISTOLA HAITCH NON EST IN ESSEX
NEC EST, AMICUS

The Letter Haitch Does Not Exist In Essex.
And Nor Should It, Mate

... as well as *this* nugget of wisdom from *The Only Way Is Essex*'s Amy Childs. She asks an important question when she says, 'Who done the dictionary, though? Is he from Essex?'

So watch out for the sections that reveal the essential local lingo you really need to know – whether you're requesting a 'vajazzle' or being heartlessly 'binned'.

Here are a few phrases to get us started:

MAYJA – a significant or important event or thing. As in: 'This situation is mayja. I'm going to call my nan.'

JELL – envious. Can be used in the singular as a question, as in: 'Jell?' / 'Yeah, well jell.'

WELL JELL – an expression of extreme envy, as in: 'I am aghast at the quality of your hair extensions, they do not look glued in at all. Well jell!'

JELL-FULL – to be full of envy for another person or thing, to covet another person strongly.

HUN-JED PAHCENT – an expression used when one wishes to concur with an idea or notion put forward by another. As in: 'Shall I send him a photo of my new vajazzle?' / 'Yeah, hun-jed pahcent, do it.'

Fact or Fiction?

Guess whether these sometimes statistical, occasionally historical and potentially factual nuggets of info are truth or daringly outrageous fiction.

For example ...

✳ ✳ ✳ ✳ ✳ **FACT OR FICTION?** ✳ ✳ ✳ ✳ ✳ ✳

DID YOU KNOW...? *If you put all the Swarovski crystals used in an average Basildon beauty parlour every week end-to-end, they would reach halfway to Saturn.*

✳ ✳ ✳ ✳ ✳ ✳ ✳ ✳ ✳ ✳ ✳ ✳ ✳ ✳ ✳ ✳ ✳ ✳ ✳

Latin Mottos for Essex

While Kent is 'The Garden of England' and Norwich calls itself 'The Fine City', there is – shockingly – no motto for Brentwood. Nor is there a Latin motto for Essex. Which is doubly tragic, given that Colchester was the Roman capital of Britain.

So as you devour the thematic chapters of this book, take yourself on a cultural odyssey and discover the phrases that might well have been said in Essex in the olden days of yore. Here's one essential motto to start us off:

GLAMOUR, SEMPER ET IN OMNI SITU

Glamour, At All Times And In All Situations

✳ ✳ ✳

Welcome to Essex.

Looking Good

Looking good is the be-all and end-all in Essex – which is why this chapter *has* to come first. Beauty and glamour are now synonymous with the county that sits proudly to the east of the capital, and it's not hard to see why.

There is a supreme amount of effort involved in every aspect of an Essex Girl or Boy's appearance, right down to the last detail. With no Swarovski crystal left unturned in pursuit of the perfect outfit or make-up job, all you need to remember is that if you've been thorough, you've been Essex.

Beauty Rules for Essex Girls

To look like a real Essex Girl, you need:

- **SPRAY TAN.** By which I mean, the full-on fake bake, and none of this wishy-washy tinted moisturizer, 'for pale skin' pathetic nonsense. If people are not asking you where you've been on holiday every time you bump into them, you are *not brown enough*.

- **FAKE LASHES.** Even for the shops. Even for answering the door. Eyelashes, *big ones*. Always. (Girls Aloud have branded some very nice ones.)

- **HAIR** – absolutely massive, cartoon hair. Long is best, preferably padded out with at least twenty different lengths of fake hair either tied, glued or clipped in. Salon applied is best.

- **GLOSS.** The lip kind. Preferably a nice nude pink. Always carried about your person in case touch-ups are necessary (they will be).

> *'A girl should be two things: classy and fabulous.'*
> **Coco Chanel,** well good dress designer

Beauty Rules for Essex Boys

To be a real Essex Boy, you need to acquire these:

- **TATTOO.** So many options, so much rippling and well-toned flesh to get inked. Ideally you won't make the mistake of choosing your girlfriend's name, because that can lead to difficulties 'down the line'.

- **HAIR.** Not for nothing is there a haircut named after the boys of Brentwood. It is The Brentwood Swoon, and it is the glossiest, shiniest, quiffiest, sweepingest haircut since Rhett Butler told Scarlett O'Hara to stop being such a moody cow. Think dye, think Clark Gable to the power of a hundred.

- **SPRAY TAN.** Not just for girls. As the saying goes, 'A pale Essex Boy is like a man without a third leg.' Think about it. And then book yourself in for a fake bake. Seriously, you look ill.

- **RIPPLES.** If you do end up getting your top off — be it in a boxing ring or on the podium at Faces nightclub — you don't want to send the revellers running to the toilets in sheer revulsion. Un-toned men do *not* win the heart of an Essex Girl. So make the gym your second home.

Essex Mottos … for Looking Good

TAN I, ERGO SUM

I Tan, Therefore I Am

* * *

**SI HOMO NON ORANGE DESTINATUM,
SCIENTIA NON EDIDERIT SAN TROPEZ**

*If Man Were Not Meant To Be Orange,
Scientists Would Not Have Created
San Tropez*

* * *

**PALE MULIER HORRIBILI CUTIS LARVA
CAUSAM QUASI TRISTES MULIER**

*A Woman With Pale Skin Is A Horrible Wraith-
Like Sorry Excuse For A Bird*

'For every two minutes of glamour, there are eight
hours of hard work.'

Jessica Savitch, American broadcaster

**FEMINA TAN NEGLEXERIT NON
RECEDERE DOMUM, NON QUIA VT
LACTIS SEXTARIUM UEL**

*A Woman Who Has Failed To Tan Should Not
Leave Her House, Not Even For Like A Pint Of
Milk Or Something*

✳ ✳ ✳

**FAKE CURSU TAN SMOOTH NUMQUAM
RUN, UNDE INSTRUCTUS COGIS MULIER
FORMOSA EAM VOBIS FACITE**

*The Course Of Fake Tan Never Did
Run Smooth, Which Is Why You Get
A Beauty Ferapist To Do It For You*

✳ ✳ ✳

'*I always have acrylic nails, spray tan, fake eyelashes.
I spend £70 a month on hair extensions.*'

Zoe Crowhurst, Romford Girl, speaking in *The Sun*

TOP FIVE

Tips for a Spray Tan

 Shave and wax at least 24 hours before tanning.

 Exfoliate and shower the night before tanning.

 Don't apply deodorant, moisturizer or perfume and remove all make-up prior to tanning.

 Wear dark underwear and loose dark clothing after the tan is applied – don't spoil your lacy smalls!

 Bring flip-flops or loose shoes to the salon for your walk/cab/bus ride/lift home.

TOP TIP

Always wear plastic gloves when applying fake tan. Once you've finished your all-over glow, add a little moisturizer to your lotion, and use this diluted lotion on your hands, knees, feet and elbows. Orange extremities are a dead giveaway!

Getting Ready:
An Essex Girl's Timetable

Getting ready to go out is a lengthy and exhaustive process you'll need to allow time for. Lots of time. And wine. Time and Wine. This is your maxim. Please allow:

1 hour

Deep, relaxing bubble bath, with time for texting your mates, swapping gossip and the drinking of wine. But don't have it so hot that your tan starts to rub off (it happens).

N.B. This is assuming you've tanned already. And waxed. Otherwise allow another 45 mins for any hair harvesting or lotion application that may be necessary.

45 mins

Dry and style hair. Remember, the Beautiful People of Essex have twice the amount of hair of an average human. The fact that said hair did not actually grow out of their own head, and was in fact put there by a hairdresser, is irrelevant.

20 mins

Application of styling and finishing products to barnet.

45 mins

Make-up. *Lots and lots of lovely make-up.* To include (but not limited to): moisturizer, concealer, foundation, lip liner, lipstick, lip gloss, eyeliner, mascara, false lashes, eyeshadow, eyebrow pencil, lip gloss, blusher, shimmer powder, lip gloss, highlighter, finishing powder, and maybe just a bit more lip gloss, it can't hurt.

20 mins

Assembly of outfit. If you haven't decided what to wear prior to this stage, then please allow at least another 45 mins for sartorial decision-making. Has he seen you in it before? No? Good.

5 mins

Re-application of hair-styling products, cf. hairspray.

10 mins

Selection and application of perfume.

5 mins

Re-application of lip gloss.

15 mins

Assembly of all make-up products to be needed while 'out'. (I have allowed at least five minutes here to search for that bloody lip pencil you put down two seconds ago, where the giddy heck has it gone, oh, there you are, but where has my bag gone ... etc.)

30 secs

Final spritz of perfume or hairspray or both. Bring it with you? *Yes.*

Total Time Elapsed: 3 hrs, 45 mins, 30 secs

> *'I love glamorous women. I'm completely behind women dressing up and looking as good as they can.'*
> **Elizabeth Hurley,** Hampshire Girl

You Know You've Overdone Your Spray Tan When ...

- The newspapers describe you as looking 'as orange as a honey-roast ham' (poor Amy).

- Immigration officials call to check your ID papers. You arouse further suspicion by asking, 'What's this? The Spanish Inquisition?'

- Your constant fear of rainfall means you donate a fifth of your wages to areas at risk of flooding.

- People start accusing you of doing 'a reverse Jackson'.

- A friend enters your living room and says, 'You've got some new pine furniture, then? Oh no, hang on, it's just your arms.'

● Your personal appearance narrows your career options to such a degree that the only job for which you are qualified is working for a certain phone company, standing outside the cinemas, on a Wednesday, as a mascot.

* * * * * **FACT** OR **FICTION?** * * * * * *

DID YOU KNOW...? *There are 100 tanning salons in the Brentwood area, and 253 in Essex as a whole. If tanning salons continue opening at their current rate, by 2050 there will be more salons than corner shops. So you won't be able to buy an orange – but you will be able to look like one.*

* * * * * * * * * * * * * * * * * * *

— TOP FIVE —

How White Are Your Teeth? An Essex Chart

 AIIIEEE, my eyes!

 Sun-dazzled polar icecap.

 Simon Cowell telling someone they've 'smashed it' / he likes it '200 per cent'.

 Snooker cue ball.

 Ivory silk.

Remember: there is an optimum contrast to be achieved here, between the colour of your skin and the brightness of your pearly whites.

If you're near the lower end of the above scale, just add another layer of spray tan to increase the contrast. Simple!

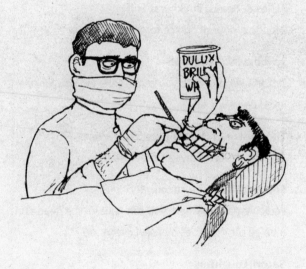

Your Directory of Essex: Where To Go To Look Good

Belles & Beaus, Buckhurst Hill

Beauty parlour of choice for all Essex Girls.

Scribble Ink, Loughton

Tattoo parlour where you can get the girl you fancy inked on your calf.

The Centre of Dental Excellence, Ware

For Simon Cowell levels of teeth-dazzle.

Sole Sensation, Hornchurch

Pedicure parlour where you can have all the dead skin nibbled off your toes by fish. Lovely!

Satori, Loughton

Hair salon for anyone in need of a girlband barnet.

Sally Salon Services, Chelmsford, Basildon, Romford, Colchester

For all your beauty-product needs, a veritable supermarket of wax, lashes and miscellaneous 'unguents' (look it up in the dictionary).

TOP TIP

Paris fashion house Balmain, which has kitted out the likes of Ava Gardner and Brigitte Bardot in the past, has recently branched out into the fake hair market ... not that there's anything 'market' about the price, with 'cashmere' hair going for a whopping £50 *per lock*.

I think it's fair to say that if you're spending this much on extensions, you don't want to be using Copydex to glue them in.

✳ ✳ ✳ ✳ ✳ ✳ **FACT** OR **FICTION?** ✳ ✳ ✳ ✳ ✳ ✳

DID YOU KNOW...? *In spiritual Essex tribes, the practice of extending hair is used to symbolize the expanding of the mind.*

✳ ✳ ✳ ✳ ✳ ✳ ✳ ✳ ✳ ✳ ✳ ✳ ✳ ✳ ✳ ✳ ✳ ✳ ✳

The Greatest Tattoo Mishaps and Misspellings ... Ever!

The people of Essex – the boys especially – are very keen on getting inked. Whether it's a picture of a scantily clad lady that covers his entire back, or a simple 'Nan' written in a cursive font, no Essex Boy goes topless without one.

In your continuing pursuit to look good, Essex-style, here are some – absolutely real – tattoo slogans you might not want to copy ...

Only God will juge me

Hmm. Not sure I'd agree with you there. In fact, I think I can feel myself doing a bit of judging, rightverynow. Terrible habit, many apologies.

Life is a choise

And so is school. Particularly English lessons. Oh dear, etc.

Poporn

Quite apart from anything else, why would you get a tattoo of a bag of popcorn on your person?

Why not? ... everyone elese does

Everyone else makes sure the tattooist can spell. 'Is this *exactly* what you want the tattoo to say?' No, no it isn't.

To young to die to fast to live

Maybe they meant it as some sort of philosophical statement. Maybe 'To die!' is the sort of thing the ancients cried when running into battle? Maybe.

Beautiful tradgedy

I will admit, sometimes I have to look up 'tradgedy' — sorry, 'tragedy'. Or at the very least, let my spell-checker take care of it. But then, I am not having it *permanently inked into my skin*.

Conqer

Maybe it is just a fancy, Top Level way of saying 'conker'. Maybe that's how professional conker players spell 'conker'. Professional conker players, that is, from a parallel universe.

Fuck the systsem

Bad enough that you wrote something on your arm rude enough to make your nan blush. Far worse that you failed to spell 'system' correctly.

Are you jalous?

Now, you could argue that they have just used the French spelling, but forgotten to put the 'e' on the end, as in *jalouse*. But you would be arguing *too far*.

Sweet pee

Maybe they like going to the toilet. One mustn't be too quick to misunderestimacize people.

Imermanence is forever

You know what else is forever? The 'p' in 'impermanence'.

Exreme

This person is so extreme, they don't need to put a 't' in between the 'x' and 'r'. Or perhaps they are an amazing language specialist and are allowed to make up completely new words.

I'm awsome

You could not make it up. Just how un-awesome a thing could be.

TOP TIP

Remember: whatever you do, spell-check your tattoo *before* you get it done. Using a computer, or a dictionary. And don't get a tattoo done if any alcohol whatsoever has passed either your or the tattooist's lips. *Ever*.

> 'We like our surgery, hair extensions, big eyelashes –
> we're very glitzy.'
>
> **Amy Childs,** *The Only Way Is Essex*

Dagenham Dilemmas

Essex Girls and Boys pride themselves on being bang up to date with the latest techniques for looking bling-tastic. So how on the ball are you when it comes to being glitter-ball gorgeous?

1. At what age is Botox the most effective?

a Over fifteen.
b Over twenty.
c Over the hill.

Answer: None of the above, as surgeons recommend not getting Botox until you're over thirty-five. But even then, caution is advised if you want to avoid a strangely robotic 'blankface'.

2. What is a vajazzle?

a The latest Hollywood blockbuster starring Will Smith.

b Snoop Dogg's latest smash single.

c The perking-up of one's lady-bits.

Answer: c). And it is not, as Harry Derbidge from *The Only Way Is Essex* (*TOWIE*) would have it, a Mexican dinner.

3. Which wax would you prefer?

a Brazilian.

b Hollywood.

c Lyrical.

Answer: As if you need to ask. It is of course b), in preparation for the application of crystals to your noo-noo. As Amy Childs once famously declared, 'Beauty is pain.'

Vajazzle Va-Va-Voom

In Essex, if you've not attended to your noo-noo, your body is a no-no.

Amy, top beautician on *The Only Way Is Essex*, tells us how it's done: 'Apply the crystals to the upper bikini area ... [pauses] ... so basically, don't put them on your actual bits.'

— TOP FIVE —

Unsexiest Vajazzle Designs

 Map of the Scilly Isles.

 Braintree FC manager Rod Stringer.

 A sausage plait.

 Your ex-boyfriend's name.

 The *Mona Lisa*.

You Know You've Had Too Much Botox When …

- You can't cry. Not even when the doggy salon applies a vile green polish to your pooch's claws.

- Your boyfriend dumps you, but you just look at him blankly until he asks, 'Hellooo?'

- Universal offer your girlband a record deal, but the most you can manage is a grimace.

- Someone asks whether the experience-based gift of a rocket trip plus a G-force thrill ride was worth the money.

- You arrive at the school gates to pick up your offspring, only for your child to say, 'I don't want to go home with the strange lady.'

- Your face is a permanent lottery win.

- You smile constantly and inappropriately — even when your nan drops a fortnight's worth of shopping in the middle of Brentwood High Street and is lightly brushed by a passing Saab.

Nan, you've been at the Botox again.

* * * * * * **FACT** OR **FICTION?** * * * * * *

DID YOU KNOW...?   *There are 106 cosmetic surgeons in Brentwood alone, with 621 in Essex as a whole.*

* *

PUELLA ISICIUM CONATUR CAPILLI
PLECTERE PERPERAM

A Girl Who Tries To Sausage Plait Her Hair Has Misunderstood

* * *

Fashion

No self-respecting Essex Girl or Boy leaves the house without looking 'hun-jed pahcent' immaculate. Nevertheless, sometimes it's hard to keep up with the competition. If you want to live it really large – and have the sort of outfit that could comfortably be described as 'mayja' – this chapter reveals all the best sartorial secrets, from the ridiculously covetable to the ridiculously expensive.

> 'We dress classy, we've got the nice handbags … It's the
> most important thing in life to look glamorous.'
>
> **Amy Childs**, *The Only Way Is Essex*

Fashion Rules for Essex Girls

● **HEELS.** If you think you can get away with flats or, even worse, flipping Converse in Essex you are quite, quite mistaken. Essex Girls do not walk, they totter. Magnificently.

N.B. 'Plimsoll' is – quite rightly – a swear word in Brentwood.

● **BAG.** *Not* an ALDI carrier bag, *not* a canvas tote, *not* the sort of bag your mum uses. What you need here is the sort of bag you could comfortably fit half your flat into. And it should weigh at least 5 kg with nothing in it, because it has taken ten cows to make it.

● **OUTFIT.** An 'outfit' is not 'a top' and 'some jeans'. An outfit is something meticulously chosen, planned and ironed (by your nan). An outfit is dressy, glitzy, hellishly saucy and should be the sort of thing you can't wear with underwear. It is *not* understated. (Understated is for girls from Devon.)

● **ACCESSORIES.** By which I mean, earrings, necklace or bracelet. Or all three together. Gold and jangly are best. You want people to gasp when you enter. But if they can't see you, you want them to *hear* you coming. Think of jewellery as being like a bell on a cat's collar, announcing your arrival to the mice. Except bigger, and golder, obviously.

An Essex Kit List: For Her

You will need ...

For everyday:

- Matching underwear in any colour other than white or cream. Mandatory: push-up, underwired bra and thong.

- Juicy Couture or Adidas velveteen tracksuit (pink, black or white, or combination thereof *only*).

- Selection of secret-support vest tops and booty shorts for 'At Home' days. An Essex Girl is never – not *ever* – off-duty.

- Uggs. Real ones, not the ones for a fiver down the market. And not the nearly-but-not-quite ones on eBay.

- A fluffy gilet for cold weather, preferably an impractical white, and preferably of the sort that

would get you mistaken for an alpaca/llama/
similarly hairy mammal.

● Skinny jeans: ideally high-end, definitely tight
enough to do lasting damage to your noo-noo.

For all-out glamour:

● A dress you can neither sit down nor perch on a
bar stool in. Think red carpet, even if you're going
nowhere near one.

● A selection of impossibly
high and totter-inducing
'taxi' shoes. N.B. Nice
(i.e. boring) Home
Counties girls think 'high'
means 3-inch heels. *You*
know better.

● A corset dress, preferably in a violently unmissable
colour, such as hot pink/red/canary yellow.

If all else fails, let this be your maxim: there is no such thing as 'too' (as in 'much') or 'over' (as in 'dressed'). As long as you remember that, you'll be an Essex Girl, babes.

> *'All girls want to look nice and we have it down to a fine art.'*
>
> **Zoe Crowhurst,** Romford Girl, speaking in *The Sun*

Fashion Rules for Essex Boys

- **SHOES.** Shiny, shiny, shiny shoes. Pointy, pointy, pointy shoes. Shoes so pointy and shiny that people who are not from Essex call you 'Winkle Boy'. What do they know?

- **WHISTLE.** Cockney rhyming slang for smart menswear: 'whistle and flute' = suit. A well-cut, preferably custom-made suit which can be dressed marginally up or down (cf. cardigans, below), depending on whether you're drinking champagne for lunch at home or in the VIP area of a club.

● **SCARF.** Tied the modern Essex way. This means you fold the scarf in half, and then loop the two ends through to create a sort of fashionable noose. It should be a designer label, and you should be wearing it whether it is brass monkeys or not.

● **CARDI.** Man cardis of the finest, flimsiest knit are very good for showing off the results of all that gym training. They also make you look the tiniest bit soft and cuddly, which is useful when you want to catch the eye of an Essex Girl.

● **WALLET.** Anyone who thinks a wallet is just for 'keeping money in' is not from Essex. Wallets are made from buffed and polished cowhide and are as soft as a peach.

● **WATCH.** If you can pick up your pint without using two hands, your watch isn't heavy enough. A Rolex is obviously what you're aiming for, but if you can't afford one, cheat and make sure that it's a) huge and b) shiny enough to blind a small dog.

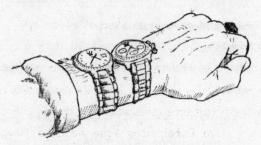

The Most Expensive Watches in the World ... Ever!

Chopard 201-Carat Bracelet Watch
£15.7 million

The most expensive watch in the world comes, as you might expect, from Switzerland and not Saffron Walden. A bracelet absolutely smothered in jewels, it features nearly 700 diamonds, including one whopping white one (11 carats), one massive blue one (12 carats) and one huge pink one (15 carats). You can't get it down Accessorize.

Patek Philippe 'Platinum World Time'
£2.5 million

Made in Geneva, this one's for the blokes. It's gold with a brown leather strap and can tell the time in twenty-four different time zones at once, including London, Paris, Cairo, Dubai, Hong Kong, Auckland, Hawaii, Mexico, Caracas, Sydney, Moscow, Rio, Tokyo, Karachi and Bangkok. It can also tell the time in Clacton.

Piaget 'Emperador Temple'
Just over £2 million (just)

French, and apparently if you press down on certain areas of the watch-face, another timepiece is revealed. So really you're getting two watches, for a million each.

The first has a mother-of-pearl dial with 173 diamonds, and the second has 688. Now, I'm not brilliant at maffs, but I make that 861 diamonds for approximately £2,322 each. Plus another quid for the strap.

Vacheron 'Constantin Tour de L'Ile'
£943,000 (ish)

First made in 2005, the 'Tour de L'Ile' (which roughly translates as 'having de laugh') is one of the most elaborately constructed timepieces the world – or Braintree – has ever seen. With 834 parts and two (what, only two?) time zones, it comes with a hand-sewn strap made of alligator skin and a buckle fashioned from pink gold, and also gives you 'sunset time', a perpetual calendar and an astronomical graphic of the night sky.

For that money, though, you would also expect it to tell you when it was 'chucking-out time', 'sexytime' and 'Chico time', would you not?

Joaillerie '101 Manchette'
Price unknown

Designed and manufactured by Jaeger-LeCoultre, the '101 Manchette' is thought to be one of the most expensive watches in the world. With a watch-face hidden behind a jewellery 'puzzle' (so it's sort of like a Gameboy?), you can tell the time by reading either the onyx, gold or diamond 'cobochons'. If you don't know your cobochons from your cheese cobs, it also has 576 diamonds and is made from 18-carat white gold.

As yet, the price of this watch has not been revealed to the general public. This is probably because if you heard how much it actually cost, you'd keel over and *die*.

'Anyone who says money can't buy happiness just doesn't know where to shop.'

Anonymous

— TOP FIVE —

Designer-Branded Products Not Currently Available That Should Be

 Toothbrush – now there's a holiday washbag worth showing off about.

 Portable hiking chair – for all that hiking in Epping Forest you're doubtless going to do ... oh.

 Crown Green bowling ball bag – for the nannas of Margate?

 Slippers – Essex people are glamorous, even at rest.

 Sock suspenders – how to make footwear garters sexier, surely?

* * * * * * **FACT** OR **FICTION?** * * * * * *

DID YOU KNOW...?   *If Essex fell into the sea tomorrow, it is estimated that it would take 38 minutes before shares in designer fashions sank to a penny a pop.*

* * * * * * * * * * * * * * * * * * * *

Essex Mottos ... on Fashion

HOMO, NEE SIMILIS ROLEX ALIQUA UEL VAGUS

A Man With No Rolex Is, Like, Some Sort Of Tramp Or Something

* * *

HOMO NON POTEST IN SOLO PANE VIVIT, UNDE FECIT DEUS LAKESIDE

Man Cannot Live By Bread Alone, Which Is Why God Created Lakeside

VICTORIA BECKHAM MULIER MEA SEDES

Victoria Beckham Is My Homegirl

✳ ✳ ✳

LORUM IN RECTE ACCOMMODATUR UT SEDEAT MEDULLA GLOBOS PER DUO MOZZARELLA

The Correctly Fitted Thong Should Sit Like A Slice Through Two Balls Of Mozzarella

✳ ✳ ✳

Essex Lingo

When in Essex, you may find yourself spending a disproportionate amount of time discussing fashion: your own outfit, what everyone else is wearing (including pets), where you bought your latest pair of designer heels (Lakeside), and – of course – what to wear next. Get to grips with how to show appreciation or abhorrence for the Next Big Thing …

LIE-KIT – an exhortation denoting approval for a person or thing. As in: 'Here, Charlie, what do you think of this handbag I purchased at popular shopping centre Lakeside?' / 'Lie-kit, Susie, lie-kit.'

LAV-IT – as above, but to be used when wishing to convey extreme approval, if not total entrancement, with a person or thing. As in: 'What do you think of my vajazzle design? Do you see, it has "Billericay" spelt out in Swarovskis?' / 'Oh, babes! I lav-it!'

SHUH-UP – this familiar phrase has two meanings: 1) please do be quiet, I do not concur with your opinion, and 2) an expression of surprise and disbelief, as in: 'I got these Louboutins for fifty quid on eBay.' / 'No, you didn't, shuh-up, you never!'

SLAY-TED – to be on the receiving end of dislike or approbation for something. As in: 'I wore the same dress two weeks running to Faces and the bouncer noticed.' / 'Oh my God, slay-ted.'

LEVVA – a rather more technical phrase, meaning the polished skin of a mammal, usually a cow, as used to make fancy car seats, suit sleeves, sofas, bomber jackets, handbags ... and Louboutin shoes.

The Most Expensive Handbags in the World ... Ever!

No Essex Girl should be seen out and about in public without a decent handbag. (And by 'handbag', I do of course mean a tonne weight of levva hanging from the crook of your arm.)

While a good high-street copy is naturally passable, here are some truly aspirational original designer items you might like to aim for. Eventually. If you don't eat for a year. And work as an investment banker. Or go out with one. Or several.

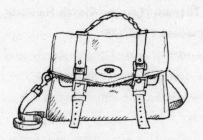

Ginza Tanaka Hermès Birkin Bag
A snip at £1,187,439

Japanese design whizz Ginza Tanaka came up with this platinum-and-diamond take on the classic Birkin bag – and used over 2,000 diamonds in the process.

But it's not just an insane designer item, oh no. Hermès say it is versatile – because in addition to being a handbag, you can also detach the diamond strap and use it as a necklace or bracelet, or use the pear-shaped 8-carat single diamond on its own as a piece of jewellery. So actually it's *intensely* practical! You should have said, Hermès.

Chanel 'Diamond Forever' Classic Handbag
A very modest £163,116

With shoulder straps fashioned from 18-carat white gold and over 330 diamonds totalling 3.56 carats, you're unlikely to come across this bag in Essex, even in Lakeside.

But that's not because Lakeside isn't brilliant ... it's because there are only *thirteen* of these bags in the *whole world*. So no chance of turning up at Faces with the same bag as anyone else! Which makes this delightful item quite the bargain, no?

Lana Marks 'Cleopatra' Bag
£152,242

Imagine leaving the lid off your lippy in the 'Cleopatra' – only *one* of these clutch bags is made each year. Designer Lana Marks's prior versions of this rare arm candy include an evening bag made from silver alligator skin, 1,500 black and white diamonds and 18-carat white gold.

Even better than that, Essex Girl Helen Mirren wore one to the Oscars in 2007, proving that you can take the girl out of Essex – but you can't stop her dangling absurd amounts of cash off her arm. Even if it's only got her fags and lip gloss in it. (Bet they made Helen give it back after.)

Hermès Matte Crocodile Birkin Bag
£74,996

Another entry in our chart of covetable accessories for Hermès, who also created this splashy version of the beloved Birkin. Boasting 10 carats of white diamonds in the clasp alone, the main body of the handbag is made from crocodile skin.

If you think that's a bit too pricey an item for your Christmas list, remember that prices for a Birkin start at an eminently reasonable £3,000. Essex Girl Victoria Beckham has at least five. The cow.

'Precious Rose' Leiber Bag
£57,497

Jewellery designer Judith Leiber creates bags in the shape of penguins, owls, kittens and, er, camels, which are completely covered in shiny crystals. The 'Precious Rose', however, is – as you might have guessed – in the shape of a pink rose. Covered with over a thousand diamonds totalling 42.56 carats and with another thousand pink sapphires and 800 tourmalines, this is one handbag unlikely to contain a lucky condom.

> *'When I got my first pay packet as a beauty therapist, I bought a Louis Vuitton and a Gucci bag.'*
>
> **Krystal Warren,** receptionist from Romford, speaking in *The Sun*

— TOP FIVE —

Things You Could Reasonably Expect to Find in an Essex Girl's Handbag

 1 Mirror.

2 Lip gloss.

3 Glue.

4 Credit card.

5 Mobile (on speed-dial: minicab, Nanna and Mum).

Glue
(and the Top Five Reasons
Why It Is Brilliant)

The humble adhesive perhaps isn't what you might have expected to find in this here volume. But upon researching the Essex people and their admirable grooming habits, it just kept cropping up. All the flipping time.

So here's why glue is so important to Essex. And why – if it disappeared off the face of the planet tomorrow – all of Essex would stay indoors. With no mirrors. And the lights off.

1. **EYELASHES.** If you live in Essex or want to be an Essex Girl, eyelashes are mandatory. Seriously, it's The Law. And you don't want to look like there's some sort of caterpillar going walkies on your cheek.

2. **HEELS.** A broken heel is a night ruined. Superglue, however, might just keep it attached while you wait for those door whores to let you into Sugar Hut.

3. **HAIR.** If there's anything worse than lopsided lashes and broken heels, it's spontaneous moulting. Glue it back in.

4. **NAILS.** Most real Essex Girls go for the full acrylic nail, built up in layers. But if you're pushed for time or money and use the stick-on kind, don't leave home without your nail glue. Otherwise you risk looking like an extra from *The Fly*.

5. **VIP AREA.** 'No, sorry, Mr Bouncer Man, I can't go and sit with the plebs, honestly I can't. No, seriously. I've glued me bum to the banquette.'

'*People think we are common, and I'll be the first to admit we are. But we know how to dress and what to spend our money on.*'

Krystal Warren, receptionist from Romford, speaking in *The Sun*

Essex Girls

The women of Essex have borne a terrible reputation for quite some time. Occasionally, it is not without justification – after all, Jodie Marsh did leave the house with two belts where her top should have been.

But what Essex girls have in common is a delightful and entirely heart-warming attitude to glamour. They *revel* in it. Nails, tan, hair, shoes, frocks and noo-noos; nothing is missed, everything is ramped up to a Jessica Rabbit-style eleven. In spite of what its female denizens might say, Brentwood is *not* Los Angeles. But Essex Girls dress as if it were, and are to be admired for this.

Essex Girls are also determined, fearless – and staggeringly successful.

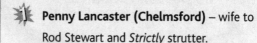

— TOP TEN —

Most Fabulous Essex Girls

1. **Penny Lancaster (Chelmsford)** – wife to Rod Stewart and *Strictly* strutter.

2. **Victoria Beckham (Harlow)** – globe-trotting fashionista and pop star.

3. **Jilly Cooper (Hornchurch)** – saucy-book-writing, pony-appreciating, Fantasy Aunt.

4. **Sam Faiers (Brentwood)** – girls' girl and budding glamour model on *The Only Way Is Essex*.

5. **Greer Garson (Manor Park, old Essex)** – MGM Studios actress, Hollywood Glamazon.

6. **Tamzin Outhwaite (Ilford)** – versatile actress and musical star of *Sweet Charity*.

Suzi Quatro (adopted, Chelmsford) – rock goddess and recurring guest on TV's *Happy Days* who resides in Chelmsford.

 Joan Hickson (adopted, Colchester) – Class Act, and the best Miss Marple there ever was.

 Sade (adopted, Colchester) – Grammy-winning, soul-singing diva with the big earrings.

 Joan Sims (Laindon) – cheeky-faced wonder of the *Carry On* comedy films.

'Essex girls may be noisy and blowsy and laugh a lot, but it's because they're cheerful, self-confident, and capable of achieving a great deal.'

George Courtauld, Essex Women's Advisory Group Chairman and the county's Vice Lord Lieutenant

Rags to Riches:
Cinderella Stories, Essex-Style

Though many an Essex Girl has aspired to find fame by treading the boards Up West, not everyone has 'made it' Up Town. These lovely ladies are the crème de la crème of the Essex Girl done good. Be inspired by the best of the best!

Stacey Solomon (Dagenham)

Former fish'n'chip shop girl who quickly captured the heart of the nation when she appeared on *The X Factor*, and then continued to charm on *I'm A Celebrity ... Get Me Out of Here!* Has the widest smile in all of telly, and a personality that is essentially that moment in *Pretty Woman* when Julia Roberts goes to the opera to see *Carmen* and says, 'Oh my God, that was so amazing I nearly peed my pants!'

Simon Cowell said of Stacey's first audition: 'I'm rarely surprised, but I have to be completely honest with you, that performance took me by surprise. I think you are really, really good.' And he doesn't say things like that very often.

'Sometimes when people think I'm annoying, I think, "Oh, I wish I could be a bit more serious,"' says Stacey. We say: don't go changing.

'I'll never keep a straight face and I know I talk too fast, I know all these things but I'm not an idiot. I'm not stupid!'

Stacey Solomon, foghorn-voiced Essex Girl

Denise Van Outen (Basildon)

After attending the Sylvia Young Theatre School and spending her youth treading the boards in *Les Misèrables* and *A Midsummer Night's Dream* with the Royal Shakespeare Company, our Denise first came to fame on *The Big Breakfast* – ably out-funnying Johnny Vaughan and becoming a firm favourite with nineties lads' mags without ever taking her top off.

Bubbly, smart, game for a laugh, self-deprecating and refreshingly down to earth, she has since starred in the West End with lead roles in *Chicago* and *Tell Me On A Sunday*. She also had her heart broken by Jay Kay from Jamiroquai, before finally bagging Joseph out of the Bible. And having his babies.

> *'They've all got 'em!'*
> **Nanny Pat**, *The Only Way Is Essex*, on Essex Girls and big boobs

Pixie Lott (Brentwood)

A product of the Italia Conti Academy of Theatre Arts, Pixie (so named because her mum said she 'looked like a fairy' as a baby) moved to Brentwood at thirteen. Appearing in theatres Up West in the likes of *Chitty Chitty Bang Bang* and *The Sound of Music*, she then recorded a demo, which was heard by Def Jam honcho L.A. Reid, who had previously signed Mariah Carey, Justin Bieber and Rihanna, and the rest is history.

Having notched up a number one for her debut single 'Mama Do (Uh Oh, Uh Oh)', she has since gone on to score another chart-topping single, a double-platinum debut album and an MTV Award. Not bad for a girl from Brentwood.

> *'The females in Faces are an exact blend of goddess and girl-next-door. Every time I turn the corner, there is some Essex honey sashaying along like some incarnation of Barbarella via Cheryl Cole.'*
>
> **Barbara Ellen,** Observer columnist

Helen Mirren (Southend-on-Sea)

Proof that age is no barrier to sex appeal, Mirren's family tree includes a Russian nobleman and tsarist colonel who became stranded in Britain during the Russian Revolution. The Communist State's loss was Essex's gain, as Helen grew up in Southend-on-Sea, attending local posh school St Bernard's.

After appearing as Cleopatra in the National Youth Theatre's production of *Antony and Cleopatra* at the age of twenty, she was quickly snapped up by an agent and has since appeared in pretty much every single play you might get forced to study at school. So pay attention, because one day it might be you picking up Oscars as if they were sweets.

> *'I think of myself as an Essex girl battling through life. How other people see me is another matter, but I can't control that.'*
>
> **Helen Mirren**, Essex Girl

— TOP FIVE —

Essex Girls Made Good

1 **Daniella Westbrook (Loughton)** – *Eastenders* actress, TV presenter, survivor.

2 **Alison Moyet (Billericay)** – outspoken and utterly fearless belting voice of eighties pop.

3 **Chantelle Houghton (Wickford)** – impossible-to-dislike, heart-of-gold-possessing *Big Brother* contestant.

4 **Martina Cole (Aveley)** – squillion-selling blockbuster writer.

5 **Sally Gunnell (Chigwell)** – javelin-throwing, sports-TV-presenting athlete of renown.

* * * * * * **FACT** OR **FICTION?** * * * * * *

DID YOU KNOW...? *Women in Essex have larger breasts than in any other county. There are 25 per cent more women with D and G cups. The other 75 per cent are still saving up.*

* * * * * * * * * * * * * * * * * * * *

Jokes About Essex Girls

Jokes about Essex Girls are invariably quite vile – as if a young woman in full control of her sexuality who likes to have fun were a bad thing. But here are some that *just about* pass muster, if you believe in stereotypes ...

What do you call a brunette Essex Girl?
A disgrace to Essex.

How do Essex Girls display their environmental credentials?
They buy unleaded eyebrow pencils.

What's the difference between Bigfoot and a pale, introverted Essex Girl?

There have actually been sightings of Bigfoot.

How many Essex Girls does it take to change a lightbulb?

None. She gets her boyfriend to hold the lightbulb and the world revolves around her.

What does an Essex Girl make for dinner?

Reservations.

How to Get Rid of an Essex Girl

Strangely, some Essex Girl jokes are a sort of meme or trope in themselves, with a seemingly never-ending number of possible answers. Here are some of the better ones ...

How do you get rid of an Essex Girl?

Tell her your Saab's at the garage.

How do you get rid of an Essex Girl?

Tell her you're skint until payday.

How do you get rid of an Essex Girl?

Tell her you like 'the natural look'.

How do you get rid of an Essex Girl?

Tell her you don't like shopping.

How do you get rid of an Essex Girl?

Tell her you're joining the Communist Party.

> *'"Essex girl" is a pejorative term used in the United Kingdom, to imply someone is a stereotypically promiscuous, unintelligent woman from Essex. It was widely used throughout the country, gaining popularity during the 1980s and 1990s.'*
>
> From Wikipedia, the free encyclopedia

— TOP TEN —

Most Infuriating Essex Girls

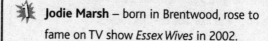

1. **Jodie Marsh** – born in Brentwood, rose to fame on TV show *Essex Wives* in 2002.

2. **Jodie Marsh** – once wore nipple pasties and a school tie instead of a top. Repeat: once wore nipple pasties and a school tie instead of a top.

3. **Jodie Marsh** – did a reality show called *Totally Jodie Marsh: Who'll Take Her Up the Aisle?* What would your mother say, etc.

4. **Jodie Marsh** – has had an ongoing feud with Jordan. Come on, girls, play nice.

5. **Jodie Marsh** – has been an agony aunt for *Zoo* magazine, and appeared in *Muscle & Fitness* magazine, for her six-pack.

6 **Jodie Marsh** – has a tattoo of Michael Jackson on her arm. Also tattooed on her arm: the A127. As in, the A127 – the road. Amazing.

7 **Jodie Marsh** – fronted an anti-bullying campaign, which prompted questions in Parliament; see, she's not all bad.

8 **Jodie Marsh** – a vegetarian, she also regularly campaigns on behalf of PETA, the animal-rights charity.

9 **Jodie Marsh** – you know, you get the impression that, one-to-one, she'd be sort of adorable.

10 **Jodie Marsh**: Contradiction in Terms. Do you know, I think I might actually love her a little bit ...

✳ ✳ ✳ ✳ ✳ **FACT** OR **FICTION?** ✳ ✳ ✳ ✳ ✳

DID YOU KNOW...? *The medieval practice of dunking women to find out if they were witches (by seeing whether they floated) resulted in significantly more casualties in Essex. The ample bosom of the traditional Essex woman tended to buoy her in the water, and in so doing, secure her death.*

✳ ✳ ✳ ✳ ✳ ✳ ✳ ✳ ✳ ✳ ✳ ✳ ✳ ✳ ✳ ✳ ✳ ✳

Historical Essex Birds

As if to prove that not all Essex Birds are alike, here are some Essex ladies from the olden days of yore. They're all dead now.

● **Dorothea Bate** – palaeontologist (try spelling that when you're pissed), died in Westcliff-on-Sea.

● **Eva Hart** – survivor of the *Titanic* disaster who lived in Chadwell Heath.

- **Ethel Haslam** – suffragette who died in Chadwell Heath.

- **Agnes Waterhouse** – witch who lived in Hatfield Peverel and was executed at Chelmsford.

- **Sarah Chesham** – Clavering-born murderess who eventually became known as 'Sally Arsenic'.

- **Matilda Fitzwalter** – virgin and object of affection for King John (circa 1212) who is said to be buried at Dunmow Priory in Essex.

- **Elizabeth Fry** – reformer and campaigner for prisoners' rights who married into Essex.

- **Mary Boleyn** – sister of Anne Boleyn, the second wife of Henry VIII, and a mistress of the king herself. Later married for love and lived in Rochford, Essex, where she died.

* * * * * * **FACT** OR **FICTION?** * * * * * *

DID YOU KNOW...? *Essex was noted for its witches in the seventeenth century. Historians have failed to establish if they actually were witches, or just a gaggle of Essex Girls boiling up some hot wax for a Brazilian.*

* * * * * * * * * * * * * * * * * * *

Essex Lingo for Essex Girls

BITS – a lady's lower regions, genitalia.

NOO-NOO – as above, a casual expression used in reference to a lady's nether parts.

YORITE HUNNY – an expression used as a greeting or salutation, similar to the more formal, 'How do you do, Madam?'

— TOP FIVE —

Essex Girls You May Not Know Are Essex Girls

1 **Juliet Stevenson (Kelvedon)** — Class Act, very good at cinematic blubbing.

2 **Dodie Smith (Uttlesford)** — darling writer of *101 Dalmations*.

3 **Dame Maggie Smith (Ilford)** — Miss Jean Brodie, no less.

4 **Germaine Greer (adopted, Great Chesterford)** — Aussie feminist and author of *The Female Eunuch*.

5 **Mary Whitehouse (adopted, Colchester)** — smut-allergic, anti-TV-filth campaigner.

Original Essex Girl: Camilla Parker Bowles

Believe it or not, some historians think Camilla Parker Bowles is really an Essex Girl. Although the Duchess of Cornwall was born in King's College Hospital, London, and educated at schools in Sussex, Kensington and – naturally – Switzerland, a closer examination of her family tree reveals her Essex heritage.

A news story surfaced in 2007 claiming that Prince Charles's ~~bird~~ wife has a few Essex skeletons in her no doubt Vuitton-filled closet, not least a distant relative whose ancestors include a cleaning woman, a factory worker and a pub landlord. And her great-great-grandfather was apparently a butler, who was born in Essex.

Maybe she should really be called Chantelle Parker Bowles?

'In the typology of the British, there is a special place reserved for Essex Girl, a lady from London's eastern suburbs who dresses in white strappy sandals and suntan oil, streaks her hair blond, has a command of Spanish that runs only to the word "Ibiza", and perfects an air of tarty prettiness.'

Michael Elliott, *Time* magazine

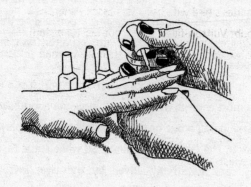

Essex Boys

Unlike Essex Girls, Essex Boys have, in the past, had a decidedly nicer treatment by the press and the rest of the nation at large. Unlike their Essex sisters, there's been no tarnishing and no casting aspersions on their willingness to hop into bed with you after too many tipples.

In fact, the list of famous, high-achieving Essex Boys is almost endless, with many a cup-winning footballer, belt-winning boxer or trophy-bagging snooker player born in The Glamorous County. So while some Essex Boys are admittedly driven by the twin joys of booze'n'birds, they're not *all* flash Harrys.

── TOP FIVE ──

Sporty Essex Blokes

 Sir Alf Ramsey (Dagenham) – footballer and manager of England who took us to the World Cup we actually managed to flipping win, in 1966.

 Bobby Moore, OBE (Barking) – footballer and gentleman.

 Nigel Benn (Ilford) – boxer. Former middleweight and super middleweight champion, who was known as 'The Dark Destroyer'.

 Ronnie O'Sullivan (Chigwell) – notoriously swift snooker player, with winnings totalling over £6 million.

Terry Venables or 'El Tel' (Dagenham) – football player and ex-manager of England, Crystal Palace, Queens Park Rangers, Tottenham Hotspur, Leeds United and Barcelona. That's a lot of kicking.

> *'My captain, my leader, my right-hand man. He was the spirit and the heartbeat of the team. A cool, calculating footballer I could trust with my life. He was the supreme professional, the best I ever worked with. Without him, England would never have won the World Cup.'*
>
> **Alf Ramsey** on Bobby Moore

— TOP TEN —

Cultural Essex Blokes

 Douglas Adams (adopted, Brentwood) — much-missed comic author of *The Hitchhiker's Guide to the Galaxy*. Famously wrote that the meaning of life was the number 42.

 Jamie Cullum (Romford) — pint-sized jazz pianist and now, Mr Sophie Dahl.

 Billy Bragg (Barking) — political commentator and protest singer.

 Damon Albarn (Colchester) — pop genius, polymath and founder member of Blur and Gorillaz. Also, dreamboat.

5 **Tony Parsons (Billericay)** – *NME* journalist and now bestselling author of books in which man crises happen.

6 **Rik Mayall (Harlow)** – comedian, best known for his role in *The Young Ones*, and as the evil Tory politician Alan B'stard.

7 **Alan Davies (Loughton)** – eminently huggable comedian and actor, him off of *Q.I.* and *Jonathan Creek*.

8 **Ian Dury (adopted, Braintree)** – charismatic frontman of The Blockheads, hero to many.

9 **Olly Murs (Witham)** – soul-singing *X Factor* contestant and pop star.

10 **Sir Robin Day, OBE (adopted, Brentwood)** – British political broadcaster and commentator.

Essex Mottos ... for Essex Boys

PONERE OUT

Leave It Out

* * *

ESSEX AN SCIT AD ELECTIONEM VEL AMARE MINGIT

An Essex Man Knows His Choice Is To Urinate Or Make Love

* * *

* * * * * * **FACT** OR **FICTION?** * * * * * * *

DID YOU KNOW...?   *The name 'Essex' roughly translates as 'Land of the East Saxons'. East Saxons have always been notoriously vain, with arguments regularly breaking out between early settlers over who could build the biggest hut, whose chattel was the fittest, and whose cart was the shiniest.*

* * * * * * * * * * * * * * * * * *

Historical Essex Blokes

- **Dick Turpin (Hempstead)** – gentleman highway robber, member of the Essex Gang.

- **Samuel Pepys (adopted, Harwich)** – history's most famous diarist and twice MP for Harwich.

- **Guglielmo Marconi (adopted, Chelmsford)** – radio whizz. The first entertainment radio in the UK was broadcast from the Chelmsford wireless telegraph.

- **Winston Churchill (adopted, Wanstead and Woodford)** – wartime leader and one-time Essex MP.

- **Edward Bright (Maldon)** – who ate all the pies? Edward did. At 47.5 stone, he was once 'The Fattest Man In England'.

- **Joseph Conrad (adopted, Stanford-le-Hope)** – novelist and writer of *Heart of Darkness*, *Nostromo* and *The Secret Agent*.

Essex Lingo for Essex Boys: Part One

GEHL – young woman or lady.

GEEZA – young man or boy, but particularly a young gentleman who might be said to stride with a certain élan or swagger.

BABE/BABES – expression of fondness for your female friend(s). Note that there need not be more than one female present in order for the plural 'babes' to be used.

PLUM – not used in the traditional sense, i.e. fruit. Instead to be used as a slight on someone who has behaved foolishly, as in: 'What are you doing calling her mobile telephonic talking device three times in one day? She will assume you love her or something, you plum.'

GOWL-DEN – an expression denoting approval, the goodness of something. As in: 'Do you know, my friend, the BMW motor cars in this here showroom are well gowl-den.'

MINT – word used to describe a situation or thing that pleases. Similar to the more formal 'Capital!' or 'Excellent!'

TADDAR, MATE – an expression to be used at the end of a conversation. As in: 'See you later, old bean' / 'Yeah, taddar, mate.'

'When you think of Essex and you think of money, good looks, tanned people and people who go out socializing who have got a good life, I can't think of anyone who's got a better life than me.'

Mark Wright, *The Only Way Is Essex*

Jokes About Essex Boys

As with Essex Girl jokes, funnies about Essex men tend to focus either on their stupidity, or on how much metrosexual pride they take in their appearance (which is hardly fair, when a hairstyle like The Brentwood Swoon has more in common with the classy film stars of the forties than with tacky Darrens spending a few quid down the dogs).

Here are some jokes that don't deserve the snip ...

Why do Essex Boys wear so much hairspray?
So they can catch all the things going over their heads.

Why don't you let Essex Boys take coffee breaks?
It takes too long to retrain them.

How do you make an Essex Boy laugh on a Saturday?
Tell him a joke on a Wednesday.

> *'He's an 18-carat nutter.'*
>
> Quote from 2000 movie *Essex Boys*

Essex Boy: Fearless in the Face of Danger

The Essex Boy will always step up to a challenge, be it a boxing match or an unattainable bird. Clacton-on-Sea resident Christopher Robinson was no different when it came to a face-off with a common-or-garden spider.

Heroically intervening to 'save' his wife, Christopher tried to kill said spider using a can of deodorant, ferociously spraying the eight-legged beast after wife Janine discovered it crawling behind the loo. His mistake was to check if he'd killed it using a cigarette lighter ... something he claimed he did because there wasn't enough light in the bathroom.

The resulting fireball explosion blew him across the

landing and left him with severe burns. 'I feel a bit of a fool,' he said afterwards, adding 'luckily I had my boxer shorts on, so I didn't get hurt in a sensitive place'.

— **TOP FIVE** —

Most Famous Essex Boys

 Ian Holm (went to school in Chigwell) – uncommonly versatile Oscar- and Laurence Olivier Award-winning actor, off of *Alien* and *The Lord of the Rings*.

 Dermot O'Leary (Colchester) – *X Factor* host, the original *Big Brother's Little Brother*.

 Jamie Oliver (Clavering) – father, chef and TV cook.

 Noel Edmonds (Ilford) – cosmic-ordering host of *Deal Or No Deal*, father to Mr Blobby.

 Ross Kemp (Barking) – nails-hard Eastender and TV presenter in war-torn Afghanistan.

Essex Goes to Hollywood

Did you spot the Essex man in *Toy Story 3*? Because there was an Essex Boy in the film, and he did the county proud.

Nominated by his son for the voice of one of the green toy army men, the 'Bucket O' Soldiers', thirty-three-year-old IT manager Mark Broughton beat off hundreds of other British fathers and was eventually chosen for the role from a shortlist of four.

So while you might have assumed he'd have been better suited to playing Ken – complete with flash car and lines to help him cop off with Barbie – our famous Essex bloke was actually the one busy saving Woody and friends.

Essex Boys and Bromance

A 'bromance' is defined by Wikipedia as 'a close but non-sexual relationship between two (or more) men, a form of homo-social intimacy'. It appears that bromances are big in Essex – if *The Only Way Is Essex* is anything to go by, where Arg and Mark seem to spend more time with each other than they do with their on/off girlfriends.

Here's a top ten of famously close Super-Bros:

1. **Ben Affleck and Matt Damon** – the original Hollywood bromance, they won an Oscar together, aww.

2. **George Clooney and Brad Pitt** – widely thought to be the longest relationship Clooney has ever had.

3. **Brody Jenner, Justin Bobby and Spencer Pratt** – three-way bromance in *The Hills*.

4. **Mark Wright and James 'Arg' Argent** – *The Only Way Is Essex*'s Team Mark.

5. **Mark Wright and Jack Tweed** – see, Mark cheats on his bros just like he does on his birds (allegedly)! At least he's consistent.

6. **Zach Braff and Donald Faison** – J.D. and Turk in TV's *Scrubs*.

7. **Jonah Hill and Michael Cera** – a bromance that seems to exist both on and off the big screen.

8. **Paul Rudd and Jason Segel** – Super-Bros in *two* films: *I Love You, Man* and *Superbad*.

9. **Frodo Baggins and Samwise Gamgee** – original pint-sized bros from *The Lord of the Rings* trilogy.

10. **Sherlock Holmes and Doctor Watson** – crime-fighting bros.

Essex Lingo for Essex Boys: Part Two

GIVVIT – to give a particular task or undertaking your full and undivided energy or attention.

GIVVIT LARGE – to give a particular task or undertaking your full and undivided energy or attention. With bells on.

OI, MATE – 'Excuse me. You there, sir.'

MANNA – the local region or environs inhabited by a person, often with territorial associations, as in: 'Gerroff my manna or I'll set the pugs on you.'

AWDA – the general state of things, the status quo.

AHTAV AWDA – expression of disdain used when the status quo has been challenged, rocked or messed with. As in: 'That gehl said my nan's sausage plait tasted of sawdust. She is well *ahtav awda.*'

BANG AHTAV AWDA – stronger variant of the above, for those situations when someone has made a grave misjudgement or error.

BANG IM AT – hit someone very hard, usually in the face, for the purposes of knocking them to the ground.

Such occurrences may well have been preceded by someone being *bang ahtav awda* (as above).

Flashy or Naughty Essex Boys

As with Essex Girls, where the occasional bird will live up to the stereotype, so it is with Essex Boys. Their alleged reputation for fast cars and even faster living isn't always unfair – sometimes it's the result of an awful lot of damn hard work, as the following, more 'traditional' Essex Boys attest ...

Darren Day (Colchester)

Love rat who left so many sad women in his wake, there isn't room here to list them all.

'A lot of people have focused on my well-publicized relationships, but of much more importance and relevance is my work itself.'

Ahem, **Darren Day,** ahem

Mark Wright (Brentwood)

Essexy chap with the piercing blue eyes. Ladies' man who can't make up his mind.

Jack Tweed (Brentwood)

Former husband to Jade Goody (RIP), former lover of *BB* star Chanelle Hayes, and tabloid regular.

Russell Brand (Grays)

Now married to pop princess Katy Perry, but previously went out with every good-looking bird on the planet. Naughty boy and all-round sauce-bucket.

> *'I like threesomes with two women – not because I'm a cynical sexual predator. Oh no! But because I'm a romantic. I'm looking for "The One". And I'll find her more quickly if I audition two at a time.'*
>
> **Russell Brand** – like I say, sauce-bucket

Dave Gahan (North Weald)

Hell-raising Depeche Mode front man.

Dudley Moore (Dagenham)

Despite his, shall we say, 'diminutive' stature, he was married and divorced four times. And all of them were knockout fit.

Love and Romance

Love and romance in the county of Essex are tricky things. I mean, it's all very well 'nicking a bird' down Sugar Hut, but the chances of you keeping them are, well, as slim as their lipo'd thighs.

Jealousy is a common theme, so watch out for green-eyed blokes who can't make up their minds if they want you – but who also don't want you to go out with anyone else while you wait for them to make up their minds. Still, half the fun's in the chasing, right?

> *'You can't have two.'*
>
> **Nanny Pat,** *The Only Way Is Essex,*
> on how many girlfriends it's alright to have

'Do's and 'Don't's:
Dating Etiquette in Essex

Unisex

Don't ... Get the name of your current lover tattooed upon your actual person. Not even if they agree to do the same for you. Not ever. A butterfly or symbol, yes. A person's name, no. And on your noo-noo, never!

Don't ... Ask, 'What's a vajazzle, then? A Christmas decoration?' in front of his/her nan.

Rules for the Birds

DO

Do ... Say, 'Ooh, that's a nice watch. Is it a Rolex? It's *shiny*.'

Do ... Compliment his car. And not just the colour. Make, model, horsepower – gen up!

Do ... Admire the threads. A suit jacket with leather arms cannot be purloined in Primark.

Do ... Admire the hair. A Brentwood Swoon is a devilish hard thing to achieve for a man, and anyone properly coiffed in this manner has taken time. To impress *you*.

Do ... Let him order. If he orders, he's paying. And Mason's in Brentwood is expensive.

Do ... Smile politely if he shows you his calf and it has a tattoo on it. Especially if it looks suspiciously like you.

DON'T

Don't ... Put your hands in his hair. You can look at it, but don't touch it unless you want half a tub of styling gel to play havoc with your French manicure.

Don't ... Arrive on the bus. Heels mean taxis, or – at the very least – a lift from your dad. There is nothing glamorous about arriving on the 551 from Billericay.

Don't ... Let him sit with his back to the wall. If anyone's going to be able to see what – and who – is happening in the bar, it's you. And it'll stop him eyeing up all the other birds.

Don't ... Drop a hair extension anywhere near your soup. Don't moult, full stop. Sudden alopecia at the dinner table is not going to give any man the frisk.

'To this day, I feel a fierce warmth for women that have the same disregard for the social conventions of sexual protocol as I do. I love it when I meet a woman and her sexuality is dancing across her face, so it's apparent that all we need to do is nod and find a cupboard.'

Russell Brand, Essex Boy

Rules for the Boys

DO

Do ... Say, 'Have you just got back from Marbella, then?' (Even if you can see the streaks.)

Do ... Compliment the frock. A lot of thought has gone into this ensemble, even if they all look the bleedin' same to you.

Do ... Say, 'Wow, your hair is *massive*!' Every girl wants to think they've got a barnet as big as, well, Barnet, and it's your job to notice.

Do ... Talk about your nan. Hearts will melt if you talk about how often your nan pops round. Just don't reveal that when she does, it's usually to do your ironing.

Do ... Pay attention to the colour of her sole. Not the ephemeral uncapturable essence of her being, you muppet, the soles *of her shoes*. If they're red, they're Louboutin (well posh and frighteningly expensive).

DON'T

Don't ... Let your eyes wander. Nothing will decrease your chances or enrage an Essex Girl like giving the impression you're checking out other Essex Girls.

Don't ... Spend any more than ten minutes talking about your beloved Colchester Town/Basildon United/Eaton Manor/Stanway Rovers FC. Even if she says she can explain the offside rule using fewer than ten words. Not even then.

Don't ... Kiss her goodbye outside the restaurant. If you think she's walking home in those shoes, you are mistaken.

Don't ... Notice if one of her nails falls off. Pretend it never happened.

Don't ... Get a vajazzle crystal stuck in your teeth. Your dentist doesn't want to hear you explain how it got there. No, they really don't.

✳ ✳ ✳ ✳ ✳ ✳ **FACT** OR **FICTION?** ✳ ✳ ✳ ✳ ✳ ✳

DID YOU KNOW...? *According to a survey, more Essex women think of themselves as 'cheap dates' than anywhere else in the UK. A staggering 61 per cent of Essex girls think of themselves as cheap dates, with 52 per cent comfortable with splitting the bill.*

Only 1 girl in 17 differed. She thought a 'proper date' should involve him spending 'at least' £150, just on her. Well, quite.

✳ ✳ ✳ ✳ ✳ ✳ ✳ ✳ ✳ ✳ ✳ ✳ ✳ ✳ ✳ ✳ ✳ ✳

'Do you know what? In my experience, the better you treat 'em, the worse they get ... and you don't want to get into a position where you're getting your melons scrambled.'

Ben, Kirk Norcross's personal trainer, *The Only Way Is Essex*

TOP THREE

Tips for a Successful Date

(From Amy Childs, *The Only Way Is Essex*)

 Don't burp at the table.

 Don't talk about your ex.

 Don't get bits of food in your teeth (especially sweetcorn ... for some reason. Perhaps they eat a lot of it in Essex).

'Essex has the lowest suicide rate in the country. They must be doing something right. It must be all the snogging they do.'

Tony Parsons, *The Sun*

Essex Lingo

NICK A BIRD – to induce a woman to commit to you romantically, quite literally to 'steal' her away from spinsterhood.

BINNED – word used to describe the end of a romantic liaison, at the request of either party. As in: 'I say, are you still seeing that darling Ramona creature?' / 'Nah, mate, I binned 'er.'

MUGGED OFF – to be humiliated in some way, especially in the field of romance. As in: 'I will not countenance being mugged off in this way. Please desist from texting your ex-girlfriend.'

MINGA – term of abuse used to condemn a woman not widely considered to be attractive.

CADDUL – an affectionate embrace between two friends or lovers. As in: 'Cam 'ere and gissa caddul.'

PLAYA – a gentleman who garners particular success in the field of romance and is found to be amiable by a number of ladies.

WURFIT – phrase used by cosmetics company L'Oréal to promote make-up, hairspray, etc. Also used by Essex denizens when another person is not worth your time or worry, often referencing playas (see above). As in: 'Who, Mark? 'E's not wurfit, babes. 'E's a playa.'

PROMISE? – ineffectual and largely pointless phrase used when asking for reassurance from one's lover. As in: 'I wouldn't cheat on ya, Sandra, honest I wouldn't, nevva.' / 'Promise?' / 'Yeah, course.'

'A clever, ugly man every now and then is successful with the ladies, but a handsome fool is irresistible.'

William Makepeace Thackeray, novelist

— TOP THREE —

Romance Tips for Blokes

(From Kirk Norcross, *The Only Way Is Essex*)

 No tongues on a first date.

 Jealousy proves that you care.

 When you're with someone, be with them 100 per cent. Until then, enjoy yourself.

Well Jell

Romantic liaisons in Essex are often characterized by one or both of the participants becoming jell-full. Turns out, there's good reason for that: the *Essex Chronicle* reports that Essex is the most adulterous county in the United Kingdom, with Chelmsford the fifteenth most affair-ridden town.

Meanwhile, statistics from a website designed to match up those seeking 'illicit encounters while still in a relationship' (makes it sound so much nicer, don't it?) show that 1,065 people signed up in Chelmsford alone.

And that's not all. Sadly, the *Chronicle* also reported that Essex falls 'well below par in the sexual satisfaction stakes' as the people surveyed gave their sex lives a rather meagre five out of ten. Oh dear.

✳ ✳ ✳ ✳ ✳ ✳ **FACT** OR **FICTION?** ✳ ✳ ✳ ✳ ✳ ✳

DID YOU KNOW...? *There's a town in Essex called Nasty, which is close to the town of Ugley. Which led to the greatest ever local newspaper headline: 'Nasty Man Weds Ugley Woman.'*

✳ ✳ ✳ ✳ ✳ ✳ ✳ ✳ ✳ ✳ ✳ ✳ ✳ ✳ ✳ ✳ ✳ ✳

Essex Mottos ... on Getting It On

ADIT MULIER ESSEX PERICLITATUR ESSE 'NICKED'

*A Woman Who Visits Essex Runs The Risk Of
Being 'Nicked'*

✳ ✳ ✳

MORSUM AMORIS NOTAM TEMERE QUIS
SIT NOTA BESTIA

*A Love Bite Is The Mark Of A Man, While A
Rash Is The Mark Of A Beast*

✳ ✳ ✳

✳ ✳ ✳ ✳ ✳ ✳ **FACT** OR **FICTION?** ✳ ✳ ✳ ✳ ✳ ✳

DID YOU KNOW...? *In the eighteenth century, the highway-men riding the byways of the south rarely bedded the ladies of Essex, for fear of comparing inadequately with the well-reputed Essex man.*

✳ ✳ ✳ ✳ ✳ ✳ ✳ ✳ ✳ ✳ ✳ ✳ ✳ ✳ ✳ ✳ ✳ ✳

Chantelle 'n' Preston, An On/Off Romance: A Timeline

Essex romances seem to be typified by their on/off nature, rather like that game you play with daisies: 'He loves me, he loves me not ...'

Chantelle Houghton, Essex Girl Made Good extra-ordinaire, and her erstwhile hubby Preston of The Ordinary Boys, certainly kept no guessing – for almost *five long years*, so hereby learn from their mistakes.

4 JAN 2006   Chantelle Houghton enters the *Celebrity Big Brother* house. Despite being a 'civilian', she quickly wins the heart of the nation.

8 JAN 2006   Samuel 'Preston' Preston (rubbishest nickname *ever*) starts to notice how adorable and kind Chantelle is. He has a girlfriend, but this doesn't stop them flirting, sometimes physically. Everyone at home can see what's happening, maybe even before the couple do.

19 JAN 2006   When Preston emerges from the house (he came fourth), his girlfriend does not rush to greet him. Oh dear. (The nation is secretly quite pleased about this.)

Chantelle beats off Michael Barrymore (dour), Maggot (who?), Preston (indie), Pete Burns (scary), Traci Bingham (placid), Dennis Rodman (grumpy), George Galloway (cat), Rula Lenska (cat accomplice), Faria Alam (went out with that geezer who used to manage England, you know, from the footer), Sir Jimmy Saville (does a lot for charity) and Jodie Marsh (Essex!) to win *Celebrity Big Brother*. A nation squeals!

26 JAN 2006 Preston gets engaged to his French girlfriend, Camille Aznar. The nation says, 'What? Noooooo!'

25 FEB 2006 Camille and Preston split up. She moves out. The nation feels it would be mean not to have at least a little bit of a sadface.

FEB 2006 Chantelle moves in! The nation has YAY on its face. It is LOVE.

25 AUG 2006 Chantelle marries Preston of The Ordinary Boys in a very splashy *OK!* magazine spread. She has gone brunette for the occasion. No one looks very comfortable in the photos. They are paid 300 thousand snickers for the shoot.

SEPT 2006 Preston tells Chantelle that he did not want to marry her. The nation doesn't know this, because she doesn't tell the nation until she is interviewed by Piers Morgan in 2008. Bad Preston. Very bad.

27 JUNE 2007 The couple announce their separation in a joint statement.

13 JULY 2007 Rumours surface in the *Daily Mail* that Chantelle is living with Preston again. The nation can't really keep up, to be honest.

21 NOV 2007 Divorce! Boooo!

24 AUG 2010 *Ultimate Big Brother* starts. Preston has another flipping pesky girlfriend. But the nation – ever romantic – holds out hope.

28 AUG 2010 Definitely some unfinished business going on. Chantelle seems keener than Preston. Darn him.

14 SEPT 2010 *Heat* magazine goes a bit nuts, and says it is buying a hat.

22 SEPT 2010 Chantelle and Preston are spotted having a cosy dinner in Battersea, London. Oooooh. Unfortunately, on the same day, *OK!* magazine runs an interview with both of them, in which Preston says he isn't sure. The nation starts to wonder if Preston is actually the MOST INFURIATING MAN ON THE PLANET.

5 OCT 2010 *Heat* magazine claims the pair signed a contract worth £120,000 to 'sell their story' after leaving *Ultimate Big Brother*. It is all lies.

10 OCT 2010 Nation GIVES UP.

What have we learned here? Mainly, that the course of love in Essex is a bit, well, on/off. If not actually a bit on/off/on/off/on/off/on/off. Similarities with *The Only Way Is Essex*'s Lauren and Mark are a bit troubling.

'When you think you love someone, set it free. If it don't come back, it was never love to begin with.'

Mark Wright, *The Only Way Is Essex*

Essex Nightlife

Essex nightclubs have become a thing of legend. And while former *Big Brother* contestants might choose the outside of a club to air their latest tabloid spat, you're classier than that.

So let this chapter be your guide to the best that The Glamorous County has to offer, from songs to get ready to, to tips on how to convince the bouncer you're too good to queue. Golden!

> *'What is a nightclub? It's boy meets girl. It may have evolved, but there's nothing that different.'*
>
> **John Clark**, co-owner of Faces

— TOP FIVE —

Songs To Glam Up To

Remember: when it comes to music, if it's 'too loud', you're *too old*.

 1. 'Material Girl' – Madonna

 2. 'Opportunities (Let's Make Lots of Money)' – Pet Shop Boys

 3. 'Gold Digger' – Kanye West feat. Jamie Foxx

 4. 'Life in the Fast Lane' – The Eagles

 5. 'Glamour Girl' – The Pussycat Dolls

'We've created somewhere special, so people behave special.'

Tony Hurrell, manager of Faces, speaking in *The Observer*

✳ ✳ ✳ ✳ ✳ **FACT** OR **FICTION?** ✳ ✳ ✳ ✳ ✳

DID YOU KNOW...?   *Essex has the oldest church in Britain, built around 600 AD. Attempts to turn it into a VIP members' bar have been repeatedly turned down by the local council.*

✳ ✳ ✳ ✳ ✳ ✳ ✳ ✳ ✳ ✳ ✳ ✳ ✳ ✳ ✳ ✳ ✳ ✳

A Traditional Tongue-Twister for Essex Girls

Try saying this after five glasses of Cristal ...

> She sells Chanel smells on the shop floor.
> She sells Chanel smells on the shop floor.
> She sells Chanel smells on the shop floor.
> She sells Chanel smells on the shop floor.

Your Directory of Essex:
A *TOWIE*-Inspired Guide of
Where To Go To Live It Large

If you want to spot some local talent, or bump into the cast members of *The Only Way Is Essex*, you could do worse than hang out in these places ...

Sugar Hut, Brentwood
Run by Kirk Norcross and
handy enough on the High
Street.

Faces, Gants Hill
Hang-out for everyone from Solange
Knowles to Charlie Uchea.

Deuces, Brentwood
Rival bar to Sugar Hut, as run by Jack Tweed and
Mark Wright.

Visage, Gants Hill

TOWIE's Candy and Michael hosted the speed-dating night here.

The King William IV, Chigwell

Pub where Sam Faiers and Amy Childs go for lots of lovely wine.

Switch, South Woodford

Where DJ Lauren Pope and Kirk do business (and nearly snog).

Bollywood Indian Restaurant, Chingford

You might see *TOWIE*'s Harry do the splits here.

Mason's, Brentwood

Where Amy went on her first date with handsome Jay. You remember, the model and, er, footballer.

'I gotta take her up one of them fancy restaurants
Up West, ent I?'

Kirk Norcross, on impressing Amy Childs, *The Only Way Is Essex*

— TOP FIVE —

Music A-Listers Spotted at Faces

 Pharrell Williams – uber-producer of everyone from Britney Spears to Kelis.

 Solange Knowles – retro soul-singing sister of Beyoncé.

 Kelly Rowland – one-third of Destiny's Child.

 Akon – chipmunk-voiced US rapper.

Ne-Yo – perma-hatted American R'n'B star.

'I'm out every night, from Thursday to Sunday. I used to go to Faces in Gants Hill. It's a place for Essex girls to show off their tans, hair and designer outfits.'

Krystal Warren, receptionist from Romford, speaking in *The Sun*

Top Tips
for Getting On the Guest List

There's nothing like swanning into a club and being given a goddess's welcome, especially when said star entrance is being witnessed by the poor sods queuing outside. Here's how to instantly up your status to A-list by getting on the guest list (all tips from www.ehow.com):

- Check online. Your favourite club might offer the opportunity to sign up to receive their newsletter, which may include info about guest lists and other discounts.

- Find out who's promoting the party you want to attend. Promoters often have their own guest lists.

- Arrive early. This may not be trendy ... but if you arrive early, you can usually save yourself the hassle of a bouncer telling you there's no guest list (or whatever the excuse of the moment happens to be). A lot of bouncers get off on giving you a hard time, especially if you're a guy. Don't give them the opportunity.

'Imagine the seventh circle of hell and you will be about halfway to understanding what Faces is like. The seventh circle of hell is the one with the river of boiling blood. Faces is like that and is in Essex.'

(Rather snobby) indie music website

TOP TIP

Why not try signing up for a guest list website? www.londonparties.co.uk claims to give you premium insider info on getting on the guest list at London clubs like Mahiki, Cafe De Paris, Embassy, Umbaba, Aura, Paper Club and Camouflage. As in, the very clubs Up West that any self-respecting Essex Girl or Boy would simply kill to go to.

Essex Lingo

UP WEST – the city of London, in particular the West End of the UK's capital city.

YOU NEVA – an exclamation of surprise or disbelief at the actions of another. As in: 'I went to the popular drinking establishment Faces, and spent three hundred snickers in the VIP area.' / 'No, you neva!'

DOR HOR – well-presented young ladies armed with clipboards, who decide if you're getting into a drinking establishment or not.

PA-CHOW – an exhortation to be used when you display your greatest dance moves or, alternatively, do the splits in public.

LAD – word used to describe a high volume of noise. As in: 'I say, would you like to go down Sugar Hut this Friday?' / 'No, thank you, one can't barely hear oneself talk in there, it's too lad.'

> *'I am a huge fan of the music here, but the girls really need to chill out, its a club, stop acting like u are a celebrity and tryin to get WAG status, and walking round like u are actually the best thing since godknows what, and dance for f*cksake!!!!!!!! dont just stand there!!!!!!! hahahaha'*
>
> Comment on Faces nightclub's Facebook fan page

— TOP FIVE —

Songs You Will Never Hear in Faces

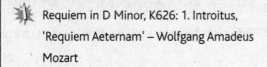 Requiem in D Minor, K626: 1. Introitus, 'Requiem Aeternam' – Wolfgang Amadeus Mozart

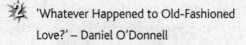 'Whatever Happened to Old-Fashioned Love?' – Daniel O'Donnell

'Where's Me Jumper?' – Sultans of Ping FC

'Heaven Knows I'm Miserable Now' – The Smiths

'Frownland' – Captain Beefheart

How to Get Into the VIP Area:
The Ten Commandments

1. Thou shalt dress to impress.

2. Thou shalt know the names of the premium vodkas.

3. Thou shalt have at least three fit ladies in thy party.

4. Thou shalt be on nodding terms with the DJ.

5. Thou shalt know the difference between 'funky house' and 'electro house'.

6. Thou shalt not be carrying thy stilettos in thy hand.

7. Thou shalt still be able to walk without the aid of thy friends.

8. Thou shalt not look desperate.

9. Thou shall strut quickly past the door supervisors into the VIP area.

10. Thou shalt not say, 'Pleeeeeease? My cousin's best mate once snogged Charlie Uchea in here!'

Remember: the guest list is gospel. And the bouncers are God.

Essex Mottos ... on Living It Large

QUEM SI TENUERIS POTUM CUM
UNDIQUE CHUCKING AGAS EORUM, ET
ERIS HOMO AN ESSEX, AMICE

*If You Can Hold Your Drink When All Around
You Are Upchucking Theirs, You'll Be An
Essex Man, My Friend*

* * *

BREAKFAST TAMQUAM REGEM LUNCH
ET QUASI PRINCIPI IN COENA QUASI
TANTUM FLUIDUM DIET

*Breakfast Like A King, Lunch Like A Prince And
Supper Like One On A Fluid-Only Diet*

* * *

QUI FATIGATUS EST TAMEN ESSEX
IMMINENTIS

A Man Who Is Tired Of Essex Is Still Hungover

'The guys just stand around the dance floor posing rather than dancing, and there are millions of girls who look a bit tacky.'

Club review for an Essex nightclub, ViewLondon website

'Do's and 'Don't's: Getting the Barman's Attention

DON'T

Don't ... Wear a high-necked blouse. It's not the seventeenth century, and you're not Abigail Williams in the flipping *Crucible*.

Don't ... Start stacking your coppers on the bar. Save it for the DIY tills in Tesco.

Don't ... Say, 'OI, MATE! OVEREEEERE, YOU SLAAAG!'

Don't ... Wave fifties around like you're a geisha with her fan. It's not 1986 anymore and Loadsamoney is oh my gawd, such a cliché.

DO

Do ... Look at the champagne menu like you mean business.

Do ... Make sure he can see your watch. You didn't buy it to tuck it under your cuff, now, did you?

Do ... Put your phone to your ear and shout into it loudly, 'What's that, Victoria? David's gone and left the loo seat up again? What a bastard!'

Do ... Smile. That teeth-whitening laser cost you half last month's salary. You're still living with your mum. Make those pearly whites pay!

'It is the early hours of Sunday morning and I am standing in a nightclub, watching a group of young women dance barefoot on chairs, with their stilettos in one hand and a drink in the other.'

Barbara Ellen, *Observer* columnist, on attending Faces

Getting Home

The *Daily Telegraph* reported that a man managed to get himself trapped inside a clothes recycling bin in Essex after a wild night out, resulting in the emergency services being called. Rescued by the fire service at 6.30 a.m. on a Saturday morning, he was described as 'drunk'.

Faaamly

If there's one county in the country where family ties bind hard, it's Essex, where a huge number of Essex Boys and Girls are entirely happy to live with their parents well into their twenties, and strong extended families mean it's perfectly acceptable for a nan to pop round to do a grown man's ironing (oh hello, Mark Wright).

In fact, it's truly heartening to see such bonded clans. Insult an Essex Boy's nanna and it might just be the last thing you ever do.

Essex Mottos ... on Faaamly Life

PLECTERE FARCIMINE SIMILAE FACIT ALICUI

A Sausage Plait Makes A Fine Meal For Any Man

✳ ✳ ✳

QUI REI ESSEX MEMINIT NATALIS IS NAN CANIS, TURPISSIMUM INDIGET ILLIDO

*An Essex Man Who Forgets His Nan's
Birthday Is A Dog And A Scoundrel Who
Needs A Slap*

✳ ✳ ✳

> *'The only rock that stays steady, the only institution
> I know that works is the family.'*
>
> **Lee Iacocca,** American businessman

Come Dine with … Jodie Marsh

Faaamly life in Essex is centred around the dinner table, where secrets are shared over pastry goods and tall tales are told as traditional dishes do the rounds. So what's dinner like chez Marsh?

Here is Jodie's menu, as seen on the hit Channel 4 TV show *Celebrity Come Dine with Me*:

Entrée:

> Poached Eggs with Asparagus and Parma Ham, served with a Sauce Hollandaise

> Poached Eggs with Asparagus, served with a Sauce Hollandaise (vegetarian option)

A panel of utterly quite pretend top chefs says: 'We are impressed with Jodie for not making her eggs look like fake knockers, when the temptation to do so must have been very, very great.'

Main Course:

Herb-Crusted Rack of Lamb, served with
Ratatouille and Garlic Roast New Potatoes

Twice-Baked Cheese Soufflé on a Baked
Portabello Mushroom (vegetarian option)

*A panel of utterly quite pretend top chefs says: 'What,
no sausage plait? How very un-Brentwood of Jodie. Also,
she could at least have called it 'LakeSIDE of Lamb'. A
missed opportunity, we feel.'*

For Dessert:

> Ginger and Orange Syrup Cheesecake, served
> with Fresh Orange Crisps

A panel of utterly quite pretend top chefs says: 'Jodie has made crisps out of oranges, which is pretty clever. No dim Essex girl is she. However, the judges feel that given Essex's reputation as the most orange-skinned county, this dish does nothing to rescue the reputation of Brentwood.'

Jodie didn't win. It was a culinary tragedy! Now, just read that menu again. Who said Essex Girls weren't classy?

'Call it a clan, call it a network, call it a tribe, call it a family. Whatever you call it, whoever you are, you need one.'

Jane Howard, novelist and actress

Make Like Your Nan:
A Recipe for Sausage Plait

Ingredients (serves 4):

8 oz short-crust pastry (ready-roll is fine)

For the filling:

Pinch of mixed herbs (oregano, parsley, thyme, etc.)

Pinch of salt and pepper

1 egg, beaten

8 oz good quality sausagemeat

2 ripe tomatoes

1 small onion

2 oz white mushrooms

To make your sausage plait:

1. Before you begin, set the
   oven to 200 degrees
   Celsius (400 degrees
   Fahrenheit, Gas Mark 6)
   – or get your nan to do it.

2. Finely chop the tomatoes, onion and mushrooms into 1 cm pieces, before adding the herbs and mixing thoroughly with the sausagemeat. All that hard work completed, you might like to sit down and have a glass of wine now.

3. Sprinkle some plain flour onto your kitchen worktop, and roll out the pastry until it forms a rectangle of about 30 cm x 22 cm. Place the pastry on a greased baking tray. Now arrange the filling in a line down the centre of your pastry rectangle.

4. Now comes the tricky bit! On either side of the sausagemeat, cut the pastry, at an angle, into 1.5 cm strips. Fold these strips over one another to form a plait that encases the sausagemeat.

5. Brush your plait with beaten egg and put it in the oven for 30–35 minutes. Once cool, take it round to your grandson's house, where he can eat it and tell you all about his latest bird trouble.

> *'Alright, Mark, I brought you some sausage plaits.'*
>
> **Nanny Pat,** The Only Way Is Essex

Funny Smell?

Sixty-five-year-old Dennis Hill, from Clacton, had the shock of his life when his house was searched by Essex police no less than six times 'because they thought they could smell cannabis'.

OAP and diabetic Dennis, who suffered two of these raids in the *same day*, said, 'I think there's a plant in my garden which gives off a similar smell.' Essex Police said they were very sorry for any 'mix-up'.

Just imagine that happening to Nanny Pat! Mark would go *mental*. She's only growing those herbs for his sausage plaits (see recipe on page 154).

DID YOU KNOW...? *The Butlins at Clacton was the second one ever built by Billy Butlin. It produces more Glamorous Grannies than any other holiday camp and competitions are incredibly fierce. Rumours abound that the finals are decided by a sausage plait bake-off.*

Dagenham Dilemmas

1. You borrow your dad's BMW M6 convertible to take your bird out, but end up tanking it into the llama pen at Colchester Zoo. At least one of the doors sort of falls off. You tell your nan. Does she say:

a 'Aw, I never liked them hairy fings. Last time me and your grandad went dahn there, they were giving 'im funny looks. There'll always be other llamas, love.'

b 'I could probably knit you another door. Giss an hour and he won't know the difference.'

c 'Tell your dad I done it. He still owes me ten grand from when he bought it.'

2. **While working on reception at your dad's gym, you accidentally give five blokes a free lifetime membership, which might just have had a teeny tiny something to do with them looking a bit fit and may – just may – also be related to them promising to get you on the VIP guest list this Friday. You tell your nan. Does she say:**

a 'It's just marketing, ain't it? Now, which one of 'em are you gonna go out with?'

b 'These blokes need all the help they can get, don't they? That's my girl.'

c 'Whatever, babes. Don't worry about it, it's not wurfit. You got any ironing you want doing?'

3. You hold an impromptu, all-back-to-mine, 'drinks party' at your nan's sheltered accommodation while she is away in Southend. One of your friends does something unmentionable – and very possibly illegal – while 'perched' on her mobility scooter. You tell your nan. Does she say:

a 'Mobility scooter, schmobility scooter. I only use it to fetch me pension and the shopping. You're still me favourite.'

b 'Come here and give your nan a caddul.'

c 'How many sausage plaits will you need between now and Christmas?'

Answer: True Essex Nans will answer with any of the above. It's in their DNA that, whatever you do, to them you'll always be perfect, deserve the best, and be absolved from all blame. You gotta love 'em!

Mini Essex

Essex Girls and Boys – believe it or not – do not spring fully formed in the aisles of Lakeside, dazzling passers-by with in-built bling and instant star quality. No, the Essex are born, not made (at least, originally, until they book their first appointment with a cosmetic surgeon).

And as it is for the parents, so it is for the children. In Essex, where glamour is your M.O., it's not just the pooches and pets who get spoilt. It's designer togs for *everyone* in the family – even the toddlers.

If your brain or wallet can cope with the following, here are some ideas for what to dress your offspring in, for maximum designer 'props' ...

CHEAP 'N' CHEERFUL
Little Marc Jacobs Striped Dress, £143
Chloé Girl's Patch-Pocket Cardigan, £173

> *'I don't care how poor a man is; if he has family, he's rich.'*
>
> **Dan Wilcox** and **Thad Mumford**, 'Identity Crisis', *M*A*S*H*

HOW MUCH?

Dior Toddler's & Little Girl's Sweater Dress, £201

Prada Patent Leather Riding Boots, £205

LIVE ON PORRIDGE

D&G Junior Jersey Dress with Ruffle Skirt, £252

Chloé Girl's Knit Cape, £271

SELL THE CAR

D&G Toddler's & Little Girl's Bow Denim Dress, £295

John Galliano Kids Girl's Silk Dress, £322

Burberry Girl's Leather Jacket, £327

> 'Other things may change us, but we start and end
> with the family.'
>
> **Anthony Brandt,** writer

REMORTGAGE THE SEMI

Dior Toddler's & Little Girl's Bow & Ribbon
   Trimmed Dress, £376

Posh Tots Destiny Gown, £389

Moncler Boy's Wool Down-Filled Hooded Jacket,
   £436

I THINK I NEED A LIE-DOWN

Baby Dior Infant's Silk Christening Gown, £822

> 'The family is a haven in a heartless world.'
>
> **Christopher Lasch,** historian

TOP TIP

Don't forget the toys, too. The Stefano Canturi Designer Jewellery Barbie is a snip at £191,500!

This one-off Barbie doll, dressed in a *Breakfast At Tiffany's* little black dress and wearing a diamond choker created by jewellery designer Stefano Canturi, was auctioned in 2010, going to an anonymous bidder in a deal that absolutely blitzed the previous record for a Barbie doll (a slightly more modest $17,091). Not one for slinging in the buggy, then.

Pets

And by pets, I do mainly mean dogs.

And by dogs, I do mainly mean handbag-sized ones.

And by handbag-sized dogs, I mean pugs. Tiny, gorgeous, cute, wrinkly, adorable pugs. That you can give pedicures and facials to!

As you can imagine, the pugs and chihuahuas of Essex are among the best cared for pets in the world; better cared for than even an Essex Boy who never has to do his own ironing. Imagine!

The Essex Motto ... on Pets

**TOTUS MANUS FOLLIS CANINI SUNT AEQUALES
SED MAGIS PAR PUGS QUAM ALII**

*All Handbag Dogs Are Equal, But Pugs Are
More Equal Than Others*

* * *

Top Tips for Handbag Pooches

Rough and Tumble

Be warned: chihuahuas are not hardy beasts. They can actually be badly injured if you stand on one while wearing your Louboutins. Or even crushed in a well-meaning cuddle – especially if you're squeezing **a** bit too hard after you've just been binned.

Bossy Boots

Chihuahuas are loud and dominant and will try to run the entire household, including bossing about your other pets – and you. If you ever see your dog telling

your nan she's put too much parsley in her sausage plait, it's time to get a new pet.

Tough Training

Of all the dog breeds, the chihuahua is one of the hardest to house-train. Coaxing, raising your voice, and quite literally rubbing its nose in it will make little difference.

Threats that *will* work are a) vowing never to take it for a facial again or b) banning it from having a doggy pedicure. Cruel to be kind, no?

Sink or Swim?

Pugs are natural explorers and won't hesitate to jump in a river or pond, but beware: they are not natural-born swimmers. Pugs are heavier in the front than in the back, so they tend to sink rather than swim.

Happily, inflatable life jackets can be purchased from a marine chandlery in Hollywood. And yes, they do come in pink. With bling on them.

— TOP TEN —

Dog Breeds to Attract Essex Girls

According to research (and imagination), the breeds listed below are the best ones for attracting a hot bird. So, grab yourself one of the following cute pups and head down to Chelmsford Park for some puppy love ...

 1 Golden retriever

 2 Scruffy terrier

 3 Collie

 4 Afghan hound

 5 Labrador

 6 Pug

Saint Bernard

 Beagle

 Old English sheepdog

 Chihuahua

Amy: 'How can Ted hold it? Dogs don't have
    shoulders!'
Sam: 'Ted's not holding it, Ted's going in it!'
    Amy Childs and **Sam Faiers,** *The Only Way Is Essex,*
    discussing dog handbags

Alternative Pets

Not all Essex types have dogs as pets – and a pet boa constrictor measuring six feet in length once eluded its owner's clutches in Barnfield, Essex. After snaking (sorry) its way out of a bathroom window, the creature apparently escaped its home completely, leading to a police search.

The local bobbies described Diego the Snake as 'thick as a baseball bat' and 'potentially dangerous'. But the rozzers were also kind enough to point out that it would only eat 'small animals'. (Er, like handbag dogs! Aiiiieee!)

> *'These Essex girls are barking. They name their pets after their perfume and jeans. I've heard them in the park calling out "Levi" and "Versace".'*
>
> Comment on an Essex nightclub forum

> 'A girl's best friend – a handbag dog rather than diamonds in this case.'
>
> *Time Out*

(Very Bad and Old) Essex Jokes About Pets

A man goes into a Brentwood pet shop and asks if they have any dogs going cheap.

Replies the shop assistant: 'Sorry, sir, all ours go woof.'

* * *

Where should you take your dog in Essex if it loses its tail?

A Brentwood re-tail store.

* * *

Essex Girl 1:   Oh my God, I've lost my dog!

Essex Girl 2:   This is *mayja*. I know! Why don't you put an ad in the paper?

Essex Girl 1:   Nah, that wouldn't help. My dog can't read.

* * *

Sports and Leisure

In Essex, the body beautiful is very important. This means lots of tedious sessions at the local gym, and pointless fights with rival owners of fancy bars. Things to remember:

● Gyms are mainly for checking out fit birds.

● Personal trainers are really relationship therapists (but cheaper).

● Boxing is simply another way of proclaiming just how one hun-jed pahcent gawjuss you are.

Also in this chapter we revel in the leisure pursuits of the Essex massive, which mostly involve cars, psychics, the gym, cars, the gym, cars and motors. And maybe the odd trip to the zoo.

$$* * * * * \textbf{FACT OR FICTION?} * * * * *$$

DID YOU KNOW...? *Guglielmo Marconi set up Great Britain's first radio broadcasting service in Chelmsford in 1920. The inaugural broadcast was the episode of* Footballers' Wives *where Chardonnay gets her thong trapped in her soft-top's roof mechanism.*

$$* * * * * * * * * * * * * * * * * * *$$

> 'It's very important to have the right clothing to exercise in. If you throw on an old T-shirt or sweats, it's not inspiring for your workout.'
>
> **Cheryl Tiegs,** well fit US model

The Ten Commandments: At the Gym

For the Birds

1. Thou shalt only join gyms that have a celebrity or footballer Members' List.

2. Thou shalt not go to the gym to exert thyself, but to get noticed. ESSEX GIRLS DO NOT SWEAT.

3. Thou shalt not need a sports bra, so thou shalt not wear one.

4. Thou shalt scour the Internet for trainers with heels. Or commission Adidas to make some.

5. Thou shalt not learn how the machinery works, no matter how many times thy personal trainer shows thou.

6. Thou shalt feign injury on occasions, in order to attract the attention of thy favourite fit bloke.

7. Thou shalt never slip into athletic mode, even if thou were Brentwood Junior Table Tennis Champion in 1996.

8. Thou shalt attire thyself in sportswear of the premium variety.

9. Thou shalt not wear thy baggy grey T-shirt left in thy flat by thy ex-boyfriend.

10. Thou shalt always keep thy trainers looking box-fresh.

'I don't exercise. If God had wanted me to bend over, he would have put diamonds on the floor.'

Joan Rivers, comedian

For the Blokes

1. Thou shalt always arrive at the gym in thy BMW or Mercedes if thy Porsche is in thy garage being fixed by thy lackeys.

2. Thy trainers shall always be as pristine as the day thou bought them.

3. Thou shalt sweat thyself dry until the dead lift is perfected.

4. Thou shalt knock the living daylights out of the punchbag to the vibrant tones of shiny R'n'B, preferably thy homeboy, Usher.

5. Thou shalt not compete with footballers.

6. Thou shalt always listen to thy trainer when having relationship problems.

7. Thou shalt always flex thy pecs and biceps when towelling thy chest after training.

8. Thou shalt never choose the running machine next to Sally Gunnell.

9. Thou shalt ignore the hottest babe in the gym, but outperform thy gym rivals when she is around. Even if it results in thy hospitalization.

10. Thou shalt never, ever, go to thy gym with thy girlfriend.

Your Directory of Essex: Where To Go To Get Fit

David Lloyd's, Chigwell
Gym where some of the *TOWIE* cast are known to tone up.

King George's Playing Fields, Brentwood
Five-a-side pitches for talking loudly about how you once had a trial with Braintree FC.

Titan Fighter Gym MMA Academy & Dagenham and Krunch Gym Ltd, Waltham Abbey

Kirk Norcross trained for his boxing match with Mark Wright here, with his absolutely enormous personal trainer, Ben.

Masters Academy, Loughton

Boxing gym where Mark trained for his fight with Kirk.

TOP TIP

Don't forget your boxing outfit! Try Box Fit in Romford for a shiny dressing gown and some boxing shorts. You'll need a combination that shows off your fake-tanned and rippling flesh, and also coordinates well colour-wise.

Remember, too, that you'll need a catchy boxing name for the big fight. Make it good and memorable, ideally incorporating some witty boxing lingo and an intelligent play on words.

The Only Way Is Essex: A Drinking Game

Of late, watching TV in Essex has become a narcissistic and therefore infinitely more enjoyable pursuit. Playing a drinking game while indulging your inner *TOWIE* enthusiast makes for an even better night in before your night out.

While I would humbly suggest you drink your Faces Sour (Amaretto, lemon, sugar syrup and champagne, doncha know) quietly and slowly, sometimes the only response to Mark and Lauren's ongoing romantic saga is to neck something stiff.

Cocktails at the ready, because if any of the following happens, you need to take a gulp. Steady, now!

- Someone says, 'Shuh-up.'
- Gratuitous flash of boob.
- People talking in their bra and pants, for no real reason.

- Appearance of pug/other handbag dog.

- Beauty treatment (being carried out/talked about).

- Mark/Kirk grins in a satisfied or smug way.

- Someone says, 'But he's still texting me.'

- Someone drinks champagne (drink twice if said drinking is not being done to celebrate anything or is happening in broad daylight).

- Amy says something a bit daft.

- Appearance of flash car.

- A member of girlband Lola squeals excitedly.

- Nanny Pat mentions sausage plaits.

- Harry Derbidge does the splits.

- Someone asks an obviously scripted question.

If you're not absolutely ratfinked within ten minutes, you've sat on the remote and must be watching *Channel 4 News*.

✳ ✳ ✳ ✳ ✳ ✳ **FACT** OR **FICTION?** ✳ ✳ ✳ ✳ ✳ ✳

DID YOU KNOW...? *Essex has fewer Great Houses per square mile than any other county in England. But to be fair, they didn't count those well fancy ones they built in 1993 in Brentwood.*

✳ ✳ ✳ ✳ ✳ ✳ ✳ ✳ ✳ ✳ ✳ ✳ ✳ ✳ ✳ ✳ ✳ ✳

Your Directory of Essex: Where To Go for Your Leisure Pleasure

Epping Forest

Outstanding area of natural beauty, good place to spot fit birds out walking their handbag dogs.

Angels Spiritualist Centre, Waltham Abbey

Have your cards read by Psychic Tarot Reader and Spiritual Medium Pat Pryde, and hopefully she'll reveal how you're going to marry a footballer.

City Pavilion, Romford

Restaurant and function rooms complex where you can hold your boxing match. Make sure you put the date into the diaries of as many local ladies as possible, for full-on Team You/Team Them drama.

Colchester Zoo

The perfect place to spot a rinasauruss (a large mammal, similar in size to an elephant, but with a distinctive, horned tusk).

Eastern Garage Car Sales, Corringham

Where the likes of Mark Wright try out new blue convertibles while at the same time updating their best mate on their ex-girlfriend's inability to move on.

Boy Racer

A number plate reading 'ESS 3X' was auctioned by the DVLA at Whittlebury Hall in Northamptonshire in June 2010. Widely publicized before the auction – and naturally of particular interest to Essex Boys, who pride themselves on having the shiniest, fastest motors – it fetched a stonking £6,520.

The successful boy racer said afterwards that he would have gladly paid another £15,000 to secure the item. Which rather puts that extra fiver you were willing to pay for that eBay dress to shame, does it not?

Essex Motto

**VENIT VENIT HORA VENIT VIR
D MERCEDES SL**

*Cometh The Hour, Cometh The Man,
Cometh The Mercedes SL 500*

✳ ✳ ✳

The Ultimate Car

The ultimate vehicle for the Essex Boy was purchased in Marbella (big shock). Bought by an 'unnamed socialite' (but let's face it, the good money's on them being from Essex), it cost a cool £1.5 million.

The Aston Martin car was heavily customized for the bloke who nabbed it (no doubt the cup holders are now the perfect size for Cristal bottles), and it's one of only seventy-seven models of the car *ever made*. It also has a 760-horsepower engine (no idea) and 12 cylinders (no, nor that neither).

The dealership where he bought it also does a nice line in Bentleys, Maseratis, Jaguars and Segways. Go and ask them for a 0% finance, 18-month deal and a part-exchange on your Golf, double dare you.

> '186 mph is the fastest I've driven – at 4.30 a.m. on the Tring bypass in a Ford GT40, naked.'
>
> **Noel Edmonds,** Essex Boy, likes fast cars. Also, nakedness

From One Extreme to the Other

The *Daily Mail*, meanwhile, recently reported a story about an Essex chap arrested by police for drink-driving. So far, so everyday. The problem was that Paul Hutton, forty, of Clacton-on-Sea, was stopped while driving a bright pink Barbie car – a battery-operated child's pink-and-white jeep measuring just 4 ft by 2 ft. He said he was trying to drive to his friend's house.

Said Paul: 'The police car came up alongside me and the officer said, "Are you all right, there?" When I tried to talk, I realized how drunk I was. A lot of burble came out.'

Hutton later admitted to being a 'complete twit'. Barbie was unavailable for comment.

The Ultimate Pleasure Ride

If gym sessions, psychic readings and motoring exploits simply don't float your boat when it comes to your leisure pleasure, why not try a naked rollercoaster ride instead?

That's what 102 people in Southend did in 2010, riding the Green Scream coaster absolutely flipping starkers. Baring all (including, no doubt, some pretty impressive 'work' scars), the thrill-seekers were attempting to break the world record for the most bare-bottomed rollercoaster riders, after a measly 32 people set the previous record at Alton Towers.

Obviously this proves conclusively that Essex is the best at *everything*.

Careers

Channel 4's *Big Brother* offered the average Essex Girl or Boy a magnificent career path that many have skipped down, hoping to find a pot of gold at the end. But now it's over.

So, failing being cast in the next series of *The Only Way Is Essex*, you might have to think a bit further afield if you want enough money to pay for that flat in Chelmsford. Pretend for a moment that you're back at school, and let this chapter be your – rather more fun and useful – Essex Careers Adviser.

✳ ✳ ✳ ✳ ✳ ✳ **FACT** OR **FICTION?** ✳ ✳ ✳ ✳ ✳ ✳

DID YOU KNOW...? *Only 10 per cent of Essex Girls list 'Doing Page Three' as a career ambition. The other 90 per cent think the real money's in marrying a footballer.*

✳ ✳ ✳ ✳ ✳ ✳ ✳ ✳ ✳ ✳ ✳ ✳ ✳ ✳ ✳ ✳ ✳

'My poshed-over voice is all learnt. My Essex girl side does comes out very often, though – I do things for the money!'

Helen Mirren, speaking in the *Mirror*

Essex Lingo for the Workplace

MODLIN – career path favoured by really, really good-looking Essex birds and blokes. Pays well, especially if you take your top off.

PAFESHUNAL – grown-up and business-like conduct, especially at work.

Which Essex Career Is Right for You?

Of course, if you really want to, you can be a rocket scientist. But let's face it, there aren't many opportunities for drinking champagne cocktails in rocket science (bor-ing). So why not try being ...

A LADY OF LEISURE

Qualities needed: laziness, hunger, the ability to pick the most expensive thing on any lunch menu.

Qualifications: BA (Hons) Getting Him To Pay, A Level Afternoon Drinking.

DO say ... *'Meet you at Sugar Hut for lunch at one, babes? Nah, me dad's giving me a lift 'cause I've got me Louboutins on.'*

DON'T say ... *'Pray tell, can I help you with any of the washing-up?'*

A BARMAID

Qualities needed: sturdy pins for standing in heels for hours, the ability to remain calm when the crowd around the bar is six girls deep and they've all just been binned by their boyfriends.

Qualifications: BA (Hons) Cocktail Composition, A Level Tip-Garnering.

DO say ... *'Can I interest you in some of our vintage champagne, sir? Seems a shame to drink beer in such a nice suit.'*

DON'T say ... *'The next person to ask me for my number is getting a Goldshläger shower.'*

A GYM INSTRUCTOR

Qualities needed: absurd levels of energy, the ability to drink protein shakes when — let's face it — a KFC would be much, much nicer.

Qualifications: BA (Hons) Muscle Studies, A Level Punishment.

DO say ...   *'Feel the burn, you wanna get out there and BANG IM OUT, Nanny Pat.'*

DON'T say ... *'Yeah, your muscles are shaping up really well. In a certain light, you could definitely pass for Jarvis Cocker.'*

'Why shouldn't young people in Essex tan themselves orange, gel their hair and seek love, sex and fame? What do they expect the working class to do? Spend our days toiling in factories?'

Tony Parsons, *The Sun*

A BARMAN

Qualities needed: strong arms, the ability to pick out the best-looking birds at the bar (and serve them first).

Qualifications: BA (Hons) Premium Vodka Brand Awareness, A Level Cocktail Shaking.

DO say ... *'Minimum spend three hundred big ones, mate. No, I said three hundred.'*

DON'T say ... *'Oh, I thought you said a jeroboam of Cristal. Oh well, it's open now.'*

A DOOR WHORE

Qualities needed: ability to withstand the cold while wearing a dress that is too revealing for undergarments.

Qualifications: BA (Hons) Clipboard Brandishing, A Level Snooty Looks.

DO say ... *'Yes, Chantelle Houghton, we're delighted you could come. Please jump the queue. Perhaps you could tell your agent about me. Hey, Chantelle! I'm a model too!'*

DON'T say ... *'If you wipe that vom off your dress, we'd be happy to let you in. But maybe you should put some shoes on first.'*

A DJ

Qualities needed: ability to wear massive headphones without looking like a complete numpty, ability to shout, 'SORRY, MATE, NO REQUESTS, YEAH?' over the sound system.

Qualifications: BA (Hons) R'n'B Appreciation, A Level Mixing.

DO say ... *'Funky electro house with a bit of hard thrown in. I'm, you know, versatile, yeah?'*

DON'T say ... *'So if I lift up the big sticky thing and put it on the big black round thing, the noise should come out of the big black boxy things. Is that right?'*

A DOG GROOMER

Qualities needed: familiarity with miniature pooches of the sort usually part-obscured by designer handbags.

Qualifications: BA (Hons) Doggie Facial Studies, A Level Application of Nail Polish (To Dogs).

DO say ... *'I love how your dog's collar matches your shoes, babes.'*

DON'T say ... *'Which one was your dog again? And was it this colour when you brought it in? Ah.'*

'Jordan is definitely my idol: her looks, her career, her businesses, she's fantastic!'

Amy Childs, *The Only Way Is Essex*

A GLAMOUR MODEL

Qualities needed: girl-next-door smile, big hair, an absolutely supreme set of knockers.

Qualifications: BA (Hons) Nudity, A Level Pouting.

DO say ... *'The Samantha Bond agency is like a Swiss finishing school for girls who like to take their top off.'*

DON'T say ... *'Sorry, completely forgot to get waxed this week. Do you mind if I just wear these tweed long johns?'*

'To get on Page Three is like playing for Chelsea. That's an achievement!'

Maria Fowler, The Only Way Is Essex

A BEAUTICIAN

Qualities needed: soft, nimble hands, an appreciation of glamour in all its many manifestations, the ability to remain smiley and upbeat when faced with a whole day of back, crack 'n' sack bookings.

Qualifications: BA (Hons) Orange Appreciation Studies, A Level History of Eyelashes.

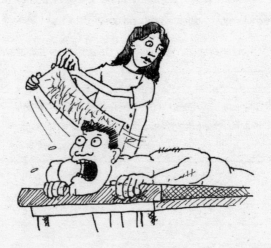

DO say ... *'I'm going to make you so tanned that when you stand in front of the Easyjet logo, you'll be completely invisible.'*

DON'T say ... *'Oh, sorry, I thought you said you didn't want any eyebrows at all.'*

A TATTOO ARTIST

Qualities needed: a steady hand, a vague ability to draw, impeccable literacy and spelling skills.

Qualifications: BA (Hons) Art & Design, A Level Cursive Script.

DO say ... *'I'm gonna make you look like Justin Timberlake crossed with David Beckham.'*

DON'T say ... *'So this bird, you said her name was Emmag, right? Oh.'*

A POP STAR

Qualities needed: adaptability (look at Madonna), the ability to dance and sing at the same time. Or lip sync and dance. Whatever.

Qualifications: BA (Hons) Modern Dance, A Level Songwriting.

DO say ...   *'I can sing more octaves than Mariah Carey and yet do not require a basket of puppies everywhere I go.'*

DON'T say ...   *'Cheryl Cole once said I had the voice of an angel. Or was it angle? I forget.'*

'I just used to write it in my diary every night; I used to write it at the bottom of every single entry, every single day. "Please God, let me be a pop star."'

Jessica Wright, *The Only Way Is Essex*

A NANNA

Qualities needed: endless patience, ability to sort out the complicated and ever-changing love lives of your grandchildren.

Qualifications: BA (Hons) Household Management, A Level Bread Pudding.

DO say ... *'Alright, babes, I brought you some sausage plaits. Any ironing you want doing?'*

DON'T say ... *'She looks like a right fackin trollop. I'm sorry, but she does.'*

'I haven't exactly got a degree in psychology, but I just love sex, don't I?'

Jodie Marsh, on claims she was 'unqualified' to be an agony aunt for *Zoo* magazine

A FASHION ASSISTANT

Qualities needed: familiarity with all the Paris fashion houses (or, alternatively, them well expensive shops in Brentwood), ability to spot potential models (i.e. fit blokes) on any Essex high street.

Qualifications: BA (Hons) Fashion Design, A Level Strut.

DO say ...   *'Babes, I can guarantee to get Pixie Lott to wear your dress at the VMAs.'*

DON'T say ...   *'Essex Fashion Week is like Paris Fashion Week except with more boobs. Those skinny, no-titted Frenchies can piss off.'*

'We live not according to reason, but according to fashion.'

Seneca, Roman philosopher from the olden days of yore

A PAGE THREE PHOTOGRAPHER

Qualities needed: contact book to rival Jordan's agent, ability to remain unflustered as gaggles of absurdly beautiful young women cast aside their underwear.

Qualifications: BA (Hons) Photography, A Level Non-Pervy Encouragement.

DO say ... *'Do you know, you ain't half got a look of Keeley Hazell. Except with better knockers, of course.'*

DON'T say ... *'Blimey! You'll have someone's eyes out with them, love.'*

Holibobs

After all that boxing, driving around in flash cars, waxing, partying, lunching, snogging and a little bit of working, the average Essex Girl or Boy is in need of a holiday, or 'holibobs'. And the whole process is very simple, as there are only two options.

You are either staying in Essex and going to Saafend, or you are 'Goin' Spain' to Marbella. So that's Marbella: The Essex of Spain, or Saafend: The Spain of Essex. (See, I told you it was simple.)

> *'Is India hot?'*
>
> **Harry Derbidge,** *The Only Way Is Essex*

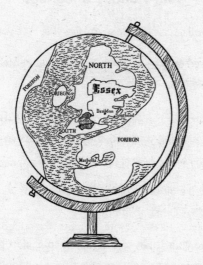

* * * * * * **FACT** OR **FICTION?** * * * * * *

DID YOU KNOW...? *Essex has the longest pier in the United Kingdom, in Southend.*

* *

The Essex Abroad:
Your Holiday Checklist

Before you get on the plane to Marbella, have you:

- worked out the distance between your hotel and Lineker's Bar? Do it now.

- looked up the number of a local taxi firm? (Unless you're taking your dad, there are no 'lifts' in Spain.)

- packed a different bikini for every day of your holiday? Don't go, if not.

- called your credit card company to a) alert them to the fact that you are about to spend terrifying amounts of cash on i) cocktails with Cristal in them, and ii) clothes, and also b) increase your limit, a teeny tiny bit?

- had a spray tan that even Chantelle Houghton would deem 'a bit much'? Remember: you are not going to Marbella to get brown, you are going to Marbella to get *more brown*.

- rung the papers? No? How are they meant to photograph you, poolside, if they don't know you're there? Sod the cabinet reshuffle, call the news desk.

- found a local restaurant that will make you a sausage plait if you get homesick? Also, who's going to do your ironing? Alright, maybe just pack your nan, she's only little, she can sleep on the sofa.

- told your mum/dad/brother/sister to look inside that handbag in the wardrobe, the big one? Because there might be a dog in it, and it might be hungry.

— TOP TEN —

Celebrity Marbella Holidaymakers Your Nan Will Remember

1. Cary Grant

2. Gary Cooper

3. Stewart Granger

4. Grace Kelly

5. Omar Sharif

6. Deborah Kerr

7. Audrey Hepburn

8. Sean Connery

9. Honor Blackman

10. Richard Burton

TOP TEN

Current Celebrity Marbella Holidaymakers

1. The Beckhams
2. Cheryl Cole
3. Danielle Lloyd
4. Craig David
5. Lacey Turner
6. Kate Moss
7. Prince Harry
8. Simon Cowell
9. Jack Tweed
10. Natasha Hamilton

✳ ✳ ✳ ✳ ✳ ✳ **FACT** OR **FICTION?** ✳ ✳ ✳ ✳ ✳ ✳

DID YOU KNOW...? *Essex has the longest coastline in the UK, which stretches for 350 miles. Things that have washed up on the Essex shoreline include 135 Ugg boots, 37,455 acrylic nails and at least 2 Swarovski vajazzle crystals.*

✳ ✳ ✳ ✳ ✳ ✳ ✳ ✳ ✳ ✳ ✳ ✳ ✳ ✳ ✳ ✳ ✳ ✳

The Essex Abroad:
A (Shonky) Spanish Phrase Book

SOCIAL SPANISH ...

Se me están haciendo muy celoso.
  You are making me well jell.

      Si-lencio
      Shuh-up.

      Oh mi Dios!
      Oh my God!

SHOPPING IN MARBELLA ...

Wow, su equipo es importante.
¿Dónde lo consigo?

Wow, your outfit is major.
Where did you get it?

✳ ✳ ✳

Quiero comprar un reloj ridículamente
caro. ¿Dónde se encuentra más cercano
emporio joyas?

I wish to purchase a ludicrously expensive
watch. Where is your nearest jewellery
emporium?

✳ ✳ ✳

Mi pájaro quiere saber donde comprar tu
bikini tanga. Quiero darle mi número. Por
favor, ¿puedes ayudarme?

My bird wants to know where you
purchased your thong bikini. I want to
give you my number.
Please can you help us?

LOOKING GOOD ...

Por favor, ¿me pueden ayudar? Sólo he pasado ocho horas en una tumbona en la actualidad. ¿Dónde está tu tienda más cercana de bronceado?

Please can you help me? I have only spent eight hours on a sunlounger today. Where is your nearest tanning shop?

* * *

Mis extensiones se encuentran en peligro de caer en mis sangría. Por favor, ¿me puedes directo a su más cercano salón de belleza de alta gama?

My extensions are in danger of falling into my sangria. Please can you direct me to your nearest high-end beauty salon?

NIGHTLIFE ...

¿Sirven Cristal en esta lista? Me gustaría comprar un Jeroboam.

Do you serve Cristal here? I should like to purchase a jeroboam.

***

Por favor, ¿me puedes directo a la zona VIP?¿Qué quieres decir, no hay uno?

Please can you direct me to the VIP area? What do you mean, there isn't one?

***

> *'All the traditional seaside pleasures, as well as dazzling nightlife.'*
>
> Southend official tourist information website, on Southend

AT THE HOTEL ...

*Por favor, ¿me puede decir cuánto va a costar
para que presione mis camisas de vestir? Sé que
tengo veinticinco, pero no puede funcionar
la plancha.*

**Please can you tell me how much it will cost
for you to press my dress shirts? I know I am
twenty-five, but I cannot operate an iron.**

Acknowledgements

I would not have written this book if I did not admire the ladies of the county of Essex – from the fabulous glamour of bygone heroines like Greer Garson to modern-day Jessica Rabbits like Amy Childs. So this book is mostly dedicated to them, and their tireless pursuit of feminine appeal.

But it is also dedicated to the Helen Mirren and Dodie Smith in my own family. Mum and Sarah, you are too extraorder to be borne. Thank you, I will pay you in 'wine', if not a jeroboam of Cristal. Hold me to this, for being so utterly insufferable on the subject of vajazzling, as well as quizzling you mercilessly about sausage plaits.

Hearty thanks also go to wonderful Editrix Kate Moore, the tireless, giddy publicity of Sarah Sandland and the darling illustrations of Andrew Pinder. May all the Louboutins and shiny cars of the world be yours.

Thanks too to the following sources, which ably assisted me in my research: *Daily Mail*, *Daily Telegraph*, *Essex Chronicle*, *Heat* magazine, *Huffington Post*, *Metro*, *Mirror*, *The Observer*, *OK!* magazine, *The Sun* and, of course, ITV2's *The Only Way Is Essex*.